Saxophone & Clarinet

AN EASY GUIDE

Saxophone & Clarinet

AN EASY GUIDE

NEW HOLLAND

chris coetzee

NEW
HOLLAND

First published in 2004 by
New Holland Publishers
London • Cape Town • Sydney • Auckland
www.newhollandpublishers.com

86 Edgware Rd
London W2 2EA
United Kingdom

80 McKenzie Street
Cape Town 800I
South Africa

I4 Aquatic Drive
Frenchs Forest, NSW 2086
Australia

218 Lake Road
Northcote, Auckland
New Zealand

PB ISBN 1 84330 336 1
HB ISBN 1 84330 335 3

Publisher and editor: Mariëlle Renssen
Publishing managers: Claudia Dos Santos,
Simon Pooley
Commissioning editor: Karyn Richards
Studio manager: Richard MacArthur
Designer: Peter Bosman
Picture researcher: Karla Kik
Proofreader and Indexer: Anna Tanneberger
Production: Myrna Collins
Consultant (UK): Chris White

Reproduction by Unifoto Pty Ltd
Printed and bound in Malaysia by Times Offset
2 4 6 8 I0 9 7 5 3 I

AUTHOR'S DEDICATION

This book is dedicated to friends, past and present:
Dieter & Zanne Stapelberg, Janine Ackermann, JB Wiese,
Marisa van der Colff, Lise van Schalkwyk, Jeanni Andrag, Carine
van Rooyen, Sasha Schagen, Alicha van Reenen, Jolene
McCleland, Michelle Davy, Vanessa Tait, Charla Schutte, André
van Daalen, Arno Jones, Carina and Philip du Toit, Rouen van
Eck, Stefan Joubert, Jan-Willem de Jager, Jaco Steenkamp, Juan
Bester, Jonathan and Carol Hoole, Tinus Kotzé, Phillip Botha,
Etienne van Wyk, Desirée Rörich, Wehan van Jaarsveld,
Larissa Mulder, Nadja Opperman, Ricardo de Agrela and
Ciska du Plessis.

contents

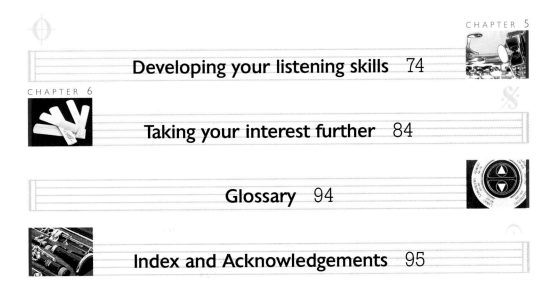

chapter one

TAKING UP SAX & CLARINET

THIS BOOK HAS BEEN WRITTEN FOR ANYBODY INTERESTED IN, or wishing to learn how to play, the clarinet and saxophone. Of course it is not possible to learn how to play an instrument perfectly from a book, but this book will give you the necessary information to help you make the various choices that playing an instrument entails.

Learning to play an instrument can be a very rewarding experience, but mastering that instrument takes time, patience and hard work. Luckily, the speed at which you progress is entirely up to you – like any hobby. This book simply wishes to share and expose you to the joys that are the result of being able to play an instrument and make music. Today's technological advances in all fields have left many people breathless, and they often seek ways to express themselves creatively in an age where creativity has been severely underrated. Some learn to paint and dance while others learn to fold their body in seemingly impossible ways through yoga. Others desire to learn to play a musical instrument. This book hopes to make your journey of discovery an interesting and hassle-free experience.

It gives you some interesting facts concerning the development of the two instruments (like the fact that the saxophone is actually a type of clarinet) and explains how they make their sound (for those interested in the scientific and technical aspects). It also teaches you to read music – which is a lot easier than most people think! You will learn how to sit, stand, breathe and play the various notes on these two exquisite instruments. This book also contains a selection of musical pieces and information on the various musical styles throughout history, the study of which can be a hobby itself. Finally, it will help you make some important decisions when you go out to buy an instrument of your own. There is a whole list of additional reading, web pages, societies, magazines and recordings to whet your appetite. If you progress enough in your playing abilities so that you'd like to link up with other musicians, there are some handy tips on how and where to find playing opportunities in bands and other ensembles.

The author, who is a passionate fan of both the clarinet and the saxophone, has done his utmost to make this book an unpretentious and enjoyable reading experience, no matter what your musical background.

OPPOSITE The ability to play an instrument, which has long been considered a social accomplishment, is an ideal way to help you unlock your creativity.

WHERE DID THEY COME FROM?

Clarinet

The modern clarinet (being that instrument we recognize as part of the symphony orchestra and forming part of the 'classical' music tradition of Western Europe) was developed at the beginning of the 18th century by an instrument builder from Nuremberg, Germany, named Johann Christoph Denner (1655–1707). The saxophone would only develop some 130 years later.

Denner devised the clarinet to produce the high notes that another instrument, the chalumeau, was incapable of producing with any great satisfaction. The modern clarinet is a combination of these two instruments: the low register (or notes) is still called the chalumeau register while the upper register is referred to as the clarinet (or often clarino because of its trumpet-like sound) register.

Benny Goodman in 1941; he is considered to be one of the most eminent jazz clarinettists of all time.

An early 18th-century engraving by J.C. Weigel of a clarinettist indicates how long ago this instrument was being played.

The ancestor of the clarinet, which looked like a stick full of holes (which, in essence, it was), differed from the modern instrument in various ways. For one thing, it looked much less complicated. Builders realized that holes had to be drilled in exactly the right spot in order to produce the correct (if any) notes. This was a problem, since many of the possible notes could not be played because the fingers of the hands could not reach the holes. A key mechanism (see p12) was developed to serve as an extension of the fingers, thereby allowing the player to play more notes than he was able to previously. Two instrument builders who greatly contributed to the development of the clarinet include Anton Stadler (1753–1812) and Xavier Lefèvre (1763–1829). As the instrument developed, it assumed a more prominent role in the musical activities of the day. Orchestras and players started using the clarinet because composers were writing music for it (for example, Mozart wrote his clarinet concerto and quintet for virtuoso Anton Stadler), and composers began writing music because musicians and orchestras were playing the instrument.

As the clarinet repertoire (works written for an instrument) increased, instrument builders redoubled their efforts to perfect the instrument since the music was becoming much more advanced and more difficult to play.

The greatest development was made by Louis-Auguste Buffet (1789–1864), who adapted the key mechanism developed by Theobald Boehm (1794–1881) for the flute, to the clarinet. This 'Boehm' clarinet is still being used today.

Saxophone

It was during this period of innovation that another clarinet maker, Adolphe Sax (1814–94) – who is seen by many as the most adventurous instrument builder of all time – developed his 'new ophicleide' (a keyed wind instrument) in 1840. It would later be renamed the saxophone. Sax designed his instrument for use in military bands, and it has kept its place of prominence in most modern marching bands. Even 'classical' composers and players were excited with this new invention. The composer, Hector Berlioz (1803–1869), reportedly said that the low notes of the saxophone made it 'the finest voice we have for works of a solemn nature'. He obviously did not foresee the advent of jazz.

Yet, despite their early enthusiasm, composers were rather slow in writing orchestral music that included the saxophone. One reason is that the strong nasal tone of the saxophone did not blend well in the orchestra, not conforming, therefore, to the musical sound-ideals of the time, which preferred that the sounds of all the instruments blended as much as possible with one another.

Looking at the slow introduction of the saxophone into the teaching plans of music conservatories (1867 in Brussels and 1931 in Paris and London), one can assume that there weren't enough skilled players to justify a huge repertoire. Another reason behind the comparatively small place of the saxophone in 'classical' music is the fact that it developed at a time when people were becoming more and more interested in 'older' music from bygone eras. Today, 'older'

Virtuoso saxophonist Charlie Parker helped change the face of jazz with his original improvisational skills in the bebop era.

music is prominent in modern classical concerts, although Berlioz and Bizet, for example, do feature in the repertoire.

Luckily, the saxophone was uniquely poised to take up a dominant role in the emerging jazz style of the early 20th century. The saxophone became so popular after World War I that there was 'a veritable epidemic of saxophone mania' in the USA (much the same as when Bill Clinton became president). This mania and the competitive atmosphere it created gave the world some of its best players, among them Rudy Wiedörf (1893–1940), Sidney Bechet (1897–1957), Benny Krueger (1899–1967), Coleman Hawkins (1904–69) and Lester Young (1909–59). The clarinet has given us greats like Benny Goodman (1909–86) and Artie Shaw (b.1910).

Even though there was a lull in activity for the jazz clarinet after World War II, it and the saxophone, particularly, came to be used extensively in rock music (notable examples: Grover Washington Jr., Clarence Clemons of Bruce Springsteen's E Street Band, David Sanborn, and Kenny G). This popularity translated into a surge of interest in the clarinet and saxophone – on both an amateur and professional level – that has kept up its momentum to this day.

The Belgian inventor of the saxophone, Adolphe Sax.

11

HOW DO THEY WORK?

Even though you're not planning on building your own saxophone or clarinet, it is important to know how they are put together and how they work. Not only does this give you insight into the problems inherent in their construction and tone production, but it also helps you to understand more advanced books on the subject. Even though the clarinet and saxophone are closely related, they are two very different instruments, therefore their anatomy will be discussed separately (except for the mouthpieces which are essentially the same).

Saxophone

The saxophone consists of more than 300 separate parts and is usually made from some metal alloy like brass or bronze and even precious metals like silver. Saxophones are often plated with various metals or lacquers. The metals include gold and silver and the lacquers can often have unusual colours like black, red or blue, as can be seen in the photograph on p8. For reference purposes, the saxophone is divided into three main parts. The body (1) houses the bell (2) and most of the key mechanism (3). The saxophone also has a thumb rest (4), but since the instrument is much heavier than the clarinet, an additional neck-strap (5) is used to take most of the weight off the thumb. The neck (6) connects the body to the mouthpiece (7) and houses the bridge (8), which is connected to the 'octave' (or speaker) key (9). The socket between the neck and body (10) is made of metal, the socket between the neck and mouthpiece consists of cork (11). Cork grease is used on the joint between the mouthpiece and the neck.

Saxophone

1. body	7. mouthpiece
2. bell	8. bridge
3. key mechanism	9. octave key
4. thumb rest	10. socket
5. neck strap	11. cork
6. neck	12. ligature

Clarinet

Clarinets are usually made from wood, but suitable plastics have made possible the construction of cheaper instruments. New wooden clarinets, which are normally more expensive, must be handled with great care in the initial months of playing as the wood needs time to adjust to humidity and temperature changes. The clarinet consists of five main parts. At the bottom you have the bell (1), which helps to amplify the sound of the lower notes. The rest of the sound escapes through the other tone-holes. Next you have the body (2), which is divided into the upper, or left-hand, joint (3) – because the left hand plays the keys located on this joint – and the lower, or right-hand, joint (4). These two joints contain all the keys that make up the key mechanism (5). The lower joint also houses the thumb rest (6). It lies above the thumb of your right hand and helps to keep the clarinet steady and in position. The bridge (7) connects the key mechanisms of the two joints. The barrel (8) is the section between the mouthpiece (9) and the body. It can be adjusted slightly to help tune the clarinet and takes the most punishment as far as temperature and humidity changes are concerned. The tenon-and-socket joints (10) between the various parts of the clarinet consist of cork. Cork grease (11) is used to lubricate the joints to facilitate assembly. It also prolongs the life of the cork and helps to produce an airtight seal.

A clarinet cleaning kit

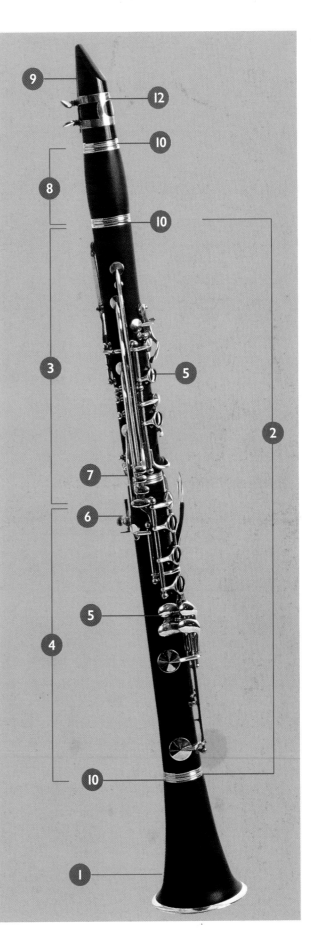

Clarinet

1.	bell	7.	bridge
2.	body	8.	barrel
3.	upper/left-hand joint	9.	mouthpiece
4.	lower/right-hand joint	10.	tenon-and-socket joint
5.	key mechanism	11.	cork grease
6.	thumb rest	12.	ligature

The mouthpieces of both instruments

The composite mouthpiece consists of a hollow mouthpiece (1), which is tapered to fit inside the player's mouth; and the reed (2), which is secured to the mouthpiece by a metal (or sometimes plastic) ligature (3). The hollow beneath the reed is called the slot (4) and the shape of this 'space' greatly influences the sound produced. The flat part on which the reed rests is called the table (5) which extends into two rails (6), restricting the movements of the reed. The rails curve away from the reed towards the point of the mouthpiece, which is called the lay (7).

Mouthpieces can be made from various materials, including ebonite, metal, plastic and even glass or crystal, all of which influence the sound.

Some information and advice on reeds

There are many different reeds and also many different makers of reeds for saxophone and clarinet, but they are all usually made from cane (although some modern reeds are made of plastic). They do not all use the same classification system, but a rule of thumb is that the higher the number (usually between 1 and 5), the harder the reed. A good way to start is to buy a few different reeds of average hardness (2 or 2½) and experiment. Each person has a different mouth and embouchure (the contact and manipulation of the reed and mouthpiece by the muscles of your mouth, tongue and face), so the only way to get a reed that suits you is to test it out. Once you find the number of the reed that you play best with, you should buy a few reeds by different makers. After you find a maker that suits your playing the best, you can buy a box of reeds. Even though this sounds weird, not all the reeds in a box are of equal quality. Playing on each reed, a seasoned player can grade them from best to worst. Even though a reed may be of poorer quality, all is not lost for it might improve with use.

Breaking in a few reeds at a time is one way of prolonging the life of your reeds in general. Play on a reed for 10 minutes, then exchange it for another. Playing on a new reed for too long will wear it out faster than breaking it in gradually. If a reed is too hard, or is not performing well, put it in water for a few minutes and try again. Make sure that you rinse the reeds after playing.

If the box of reeds did not come with individual guards for each reed, invest in a reed guard (see p90). Make sure you buy one that will fit in the case of your instrument, so that you can keep a few good reeds with you no matter where you go.

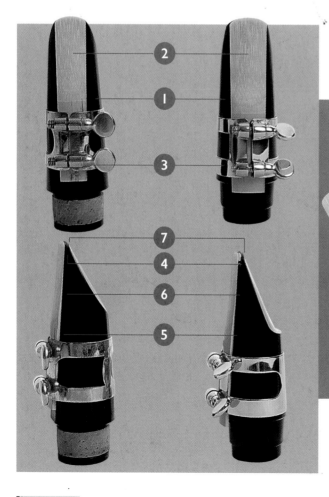

LEFT TO RIGHT Reeds for the clarinet, baritone, tenor, alto and soprano saxophones respectively.

LEFT A clarinet mouthpiece (far left, top and bottom) can be distinguished from a saxophone mouthpiece by the cork socket at the bottom. Also notice that the saxophone reed is wider than that of the clarinet.

THE SCIENCE BEHIND THE SOUND

Clarinets and saxophones are classified as wind instruments (the sound is produced by your own 'wind' – the breath). Wind instruments are divided into two categories, namely brass and woodwind. Brass wind instruments produce their sound when the player's lips vibrate against a cup-shaped mouthpiece. Woodwind instruments produce their sound through a vibrating reed (or reeds) – except in the case of the flute, where the mouthpiece is built to disturb the air stream and cause a regular vibration. This is why the saxophone is classified as a woodwind instrument: it may be made of brass, but a vibrating reed produces the sound – which is what sound is: vibrations in the air. If these vibrations, which are measured in hertz (beats per second), are regular, a stable pitch will result. The pitch to which a symphony orchestra tunes is called concert A 440 – the note is produced when the vibrations are constant at 440 vibrations per second.

Wind instruments can be described as vibrating columns of air. The larger (or longer) the instrument, the slower the vibrations, the lower the sound. The smaller (or shorter) the instrument, the faster the vibrations, the higher the sound. This is why these instruments have all their holes and keys – to lengthen and shorten the air column, thereby changing the vibrations and the note produced, making it possible to produce many different notes.

Since one is unable to play all possible notes on one instrument, several sizes of the same instrument were developed so that you could play as many different notes (ranging from very high to very low) as possible. These sizes are described either with words that also describe the human voice (such as alto, tenor or baritone saxophone) or according to the key (see p24) they are pitched in (such as the A-, E-flat or B-flat clarinet).

ABOVE The fewer keys that are depressed, the shorter the vibrating length of the air column – and this will result in a higher pitch.

ABOVE You will notice that by depressing the keys, the pads seal the tone holes, lengthening the air column. In this way, the pitch is lowered.

LEARNING THE LANGUAGE

MUSIC IS, IN ACTUAL FACT, AN EASY LANGUAGE TO LEARN — it can be grasped in a fraction of the time it would take to learn the most rudimentary English. And if you know the first seven letters of the alphabet, can multiply and divide by two, then you know more than half of what you need! However, it has to be practised on a daily basis for it to have any benefit — after all, it's not possible to speak a language unless you practise it often.

The notes that the composer hears in his head are pinned to the page (much like a collector will pin down an elusive butterfly) using a system known as staff notation. This system tries to give a visual approximation of what you hear so that it can be reproduced later.

The development of musical notation started approximately 1200 years ago. It was the mid-point of the Middle Ages and the Catholic Church formed the centre of European civilization. Daily services were held in monasteries and churches, and sacred songs, known to many as 'Gregorian chant' (but is more correctly called *cantus planus*, or plainsong) illuminated these services. These songs were chanted by priests who alternated with a choir, consisting mostly of boys and men. But as the rites and liturgy expanded, the men found that they could not remember all the melodies (there being a few thousand). Various systems were employed to remind the choir of the melodies, such as the use of hand signals. Later, since the clergy were the only literate people at the time, it was logical that they would try to write the melodies down. They started by writing down the words of a hymn, and added squiggly markings above the words, ascending and descending as the melody did. This seemed to work relatively well, but it was rather imprecise as it did not show them on which note to begin. Adding a line solved this problem. All squiggles on the line represented a specific note, while squiggles above the line were higher than that note and vice versa. More lines were added to narrow down the possible confusion over notes between the lines, until the five lines that constitute the modern stave (see p22) were formalized during the late 15th century. This 'notation' spread through Europe with the help of the Church, and it soon became a language understood internationally by most musicians.

OPPOSITE This beautifully illuminated manuscript, dating from c.1450, clearly shows the five horizontal lines that make up the modern musical stave.

RHYTHM

The value of the notes

Imagine a whole, uncut apple. Compare this to the single uncoloured circle that constitutes one whole note, or semi-breve (old English terminology). If you were to divide the apple into two equal parts, you would have two half apples. To make a half note, or minim, add a stem to a whole note. Dividing the half note equally, you would have two quarter notes, or crotchets – they look like half notes, but the note-heads are coloured in. Dividing one quarter note would give you two eighth notes, or quavers, each looking like a quarter note with a flag or tail attached to the end of the stem. A sixteenth note, or semiquaver, will have two flags. A thirty-second note, or demisemiquaver, will have three, and a sixty-fourth note, or hemidemisemiquaver!, will have four.

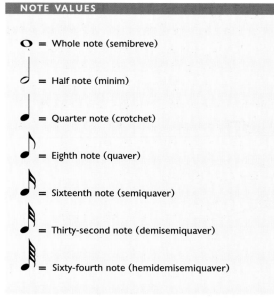

NOTE VALUES

𝅝 =	Whole note (semibreve)
𝅗𝅥 =	Half note (minim)
♩ =	Quarter note (crotchet)
♪ =	Eighth note (quaver)
𝅘𝅥𝅯 =	Sixteenth note (semiquaver)
𝅘𝅥𝅰 =	Thirty-second note (demisemiquaver)
𝅘𝅥𝅱 =	Sixty-fourth note (hemidemisemiquaver)

TIME

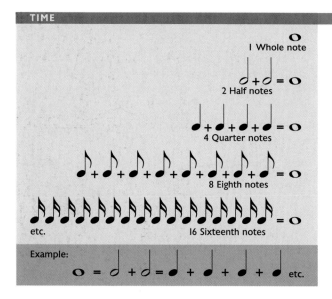

Time

Music takes place in time and would cease to be heard if time were to stand still. Luckily, it won't! Thus, one quarter note will sound just as long as two eighth notes in the same piece of music. In the same way, one quarter note will sound only half the length of one half note. This very basic manifestation of mathematics is the foundation of all time in music. It is important to understand the relativity between note lengths. Just because a note is 'larger' does not mean that the note will be necessarily slow. It could happen that a half note in a fast piece will sound shorter than an eighth note in a slow piece. The relative speed of notes in a piece is indicated by tempo indications (see p26).

The bar

This is not a place where you can order a piña colada but the space between two bar lines. A bar line is a vertical line that runs from the top to the bottom of a stave (the five horizontal lines) and can often span several staves. Each bar has a number (usually starting with one) and is the musician's means of finding a certain place in a piece of music. Two bar lines of equal thickness next to one another constitute a double bar line, which is used to divide a piece into sections. The final bar line has a thick second line and usually occurs at the end of a piece. If an entire section of music is repeated, a repeat sign (:) is used. When you see a repeat sign, you either go back to the beginning, or back to the nearest double bar line or beginning of the section.

THE BAR

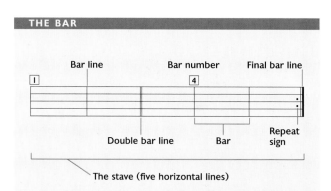

If entire sections of music are repeated, a repeat sign is used to indicate that the preceding sections should be played again, rather than duplicating the music.

Time signature

Most pieces of music have a time signature written at the beginning of the piece. It is indicated by a fraction, which divides each bar into equal beats. The top number (usually between 2 and 12) gives the number of beats per bar. The bottom number (any multiple of two) gives the value of the beat: a two signifies a half note per beat; a four, a quarter note per beat; an eight, an eighth note; and so on.

Counting the beats

It is very important to be aware of the regularity of the beat when you play. The main beats can be tapped with your foot, or you can use a metronome (see p41) to keep the constant beat for you. As you progress, you should be able to keep this beat internally, but it does take practice. This book makes use of the following system to indicate the beat for you: the main beats are indicated by a number above the notes occurring on that beat; subdivisions of the beat are marked with an + sign (pronounced as 'and', not 'plus'). The first example (a) would be counted thus: 'one and two and three and . . .' and so on. The second example (b) will be counted 'one and two

and three and four and. . .'. Practise these examples by counting out loud in the way described and clap the rhythms. This is a good exercise in multi-tasking since you have to concentrate on saying the correct words while clapping.

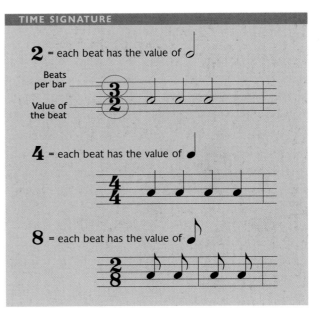

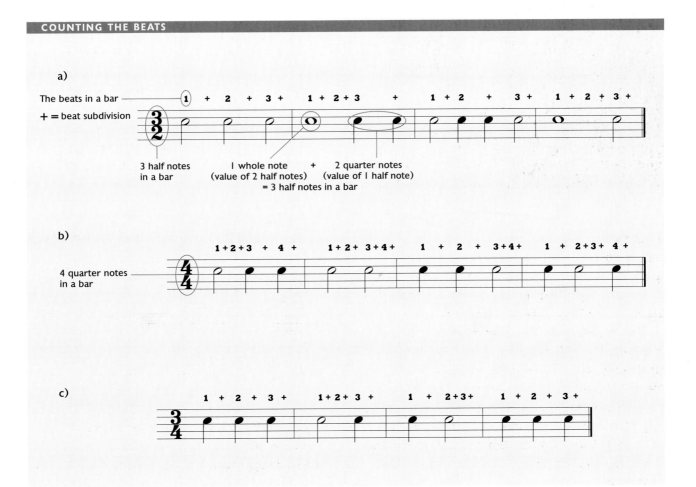

Rests

Just as there are notes to indicate when a pitch is sounded, there are rests to denote when there is silence. These rests correspond to the values of the notes that they substitute and composers use rests to allow the music to breathe (not to mention the fact that, for a wind player, this is an ideal spot to do the same). The whole note rest looks like a small, black rectangle 'hanging' from a line. The half note rest looks the same, but 'sits' on a line. The quarter note rest looks like a squiggle (or a back-to-front eighth rest), while the 'flagged' notes all have rest signs that look like a '7', with a number of vertical strokes indicating the number of flags.

One exception does occur for which we have a rule: if a whole bar remains silent, a whole note rest is used, no matter what the time signature.

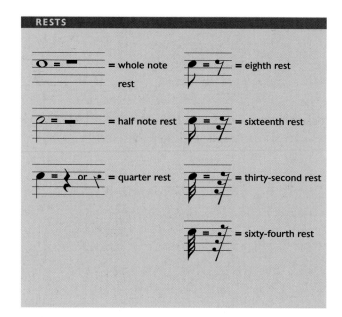

Dotted Notes

Dotted half note = one half note + one quarter note.

Dotted quarter note = one quarter note + one eighth note.

Dotted eighth note = one eighth note + one sixteenth note.

Double-dotted note = one quarter + one eighth + one sixteenth.

Dots

A dot to the immediate right of a note lengthens the note by half its value. Thus a dotted half note will be equal in length to the combined length of a half note plus a quarter note or three quarter notes. If a second dot appears to the immediate right of the first dot, it further lengthens the note by half the value of the first dot. Therefore, a double-dotted half note will sound the composite length of a half note plus a quarter note plus an eighth note (or seven eighth notes). Double-dotted notes have to be played very precisely to have the intended effect of increasing the vitality of the music. Imagine playing the second note a split second too late and you should get it right. In music of the 17th century (see p46), one often has to play dotted notes in a double dotted fashion. Rests can also be dotted or double-dotted.

Accents

In a piece of music with a regular beat, some beats carry more emphasis than others. In a piece with two beats to a bar (like a march), the first beat is more important than the second beat. Where a piece has three beats to a bar (like a waltz), the first beat is more important than the second or third. Where there are four beats to a bar, the first beat is the most important, the third beat the second most important, and the second and fourth the least important.

The sign used in music to give a certain note a particular emphasis is called the accent (>) and usually takes on the form of an arrowhead. Accents that do not fall in their natural place or 'displaced' accents are referred to as syncopation.

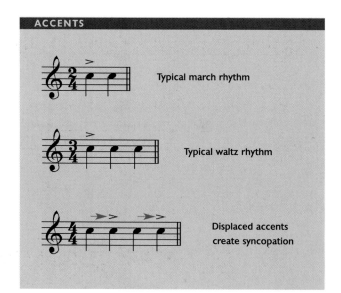

Typical march rhythm

Typical waltz rhythm

Displaced accents create syncopation

Groups

Notes are grouped in a certain way within the bar. So, if there are three beats to a bar, the notes will be in three groups (this obviously only applies to notes that are equal or smaller in value to the full value of the beat). Thick horizontal lines or beams link the notes within the same group. Only notes with flags get beamed together, with the number of beams corres- ponding to the number of flags – it looks neater than writing each flagged note separately. Time signatures with a 2, 3 or 4 as the top value are called simple times because there are only as many groups of notes as there are beats. Time signatures with a 6, 9 or 12 as the top value are called compound times because there are three beats to each group.

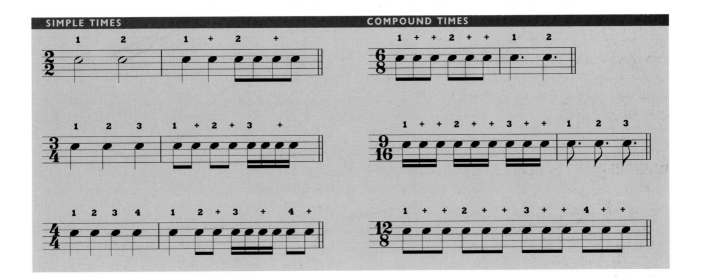

Rhythm exercises

You are now halfway in your journey of learning to read music! Here are some exercises which should help you to read musical rhythm. They can be clapped, sung or played as a single note on your clarinet or saxophone. Count the beats written above them (silently if you are making use of option number three). Make sure that your beats are of equal length.

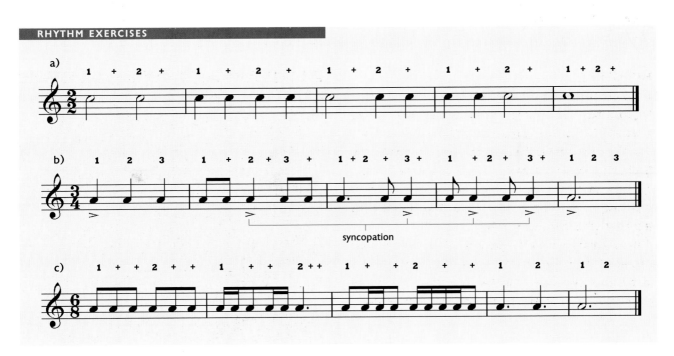

PITCH

Back to the keyboard

Since it is not possible to visualize all the notes on a clarinet and saxophone simultaneously as you do on the piano, it is a good idea to discuss the fundamentals of pitch using the piano as a model. It is also recommended that, where possible, you spend some time at a piano to test out these theories. The piano keyboard is arranged into two rows of keys, one white and one black. The black keys are consistently arranged in groups of two and three across the entire keyboard (except perhaps the extreme edges) – for a very specific reason. The white keys are named after the first seven letters of the alphabet. Every white note to the immediate right of the middle black note in the groups of three is the note A. The next white note, to the right of A, is B; the next white note is C, and so on. This continues as far as G, after which A follows once again to the right of the next middle black note. Adjacent As are said to be an octave apart (from the Latin word, *octo*, meaning eight) because it is eight white notes from the one to the other.

The stave

The stave consists of five horizontal lines. A note is either on a line or in the space between two lines. If notes go higher or lower than the stave allows, a ledger line is used. This has the same function as the lines of the stave, but is only used for the specific note.

Clef signs

Clef signs are used to specify the register of notes. The treble clef ♪ is used for notes to the right of middle C (the C in the

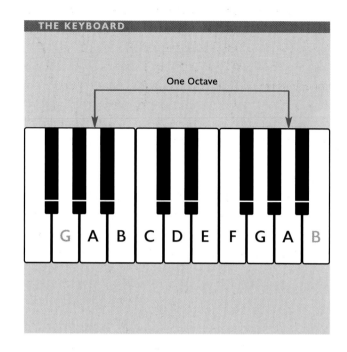

THE KEYBOARD

One Octave

G A B C D E F G A B

middle of the keyboard), while the bass clef 𝄢 is used for notes to the left of middle C. There are many different clef signs, but most clarinettists and saxophonists read only in the treble clef, so we will only concentrate on this one. In the treble clef, middle C is notated on the first ledger line below the stave (when we say 'first line' we mean the bottom one), making the note on the first line the E above middle C. When you play a notated middle C on your clarinet or saxophone, it will not sound like the middle C on the piano because it is a transposing instrument (see p24).

For the full fingering details of written notes for clarinet and saxophone, see pp36–37.

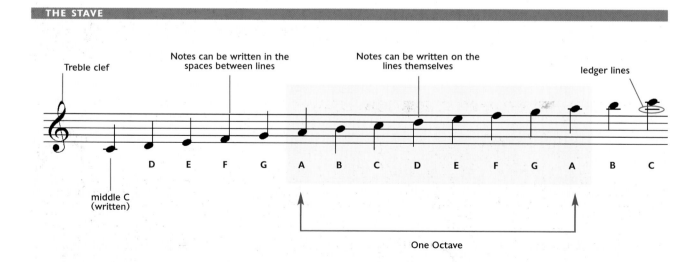

THE STAVE

Treble clef

Notes can be written in the spaces between lines

Notes can be written on the lines themselves

ledger lines

middle C (written)

D E F G A B C D E F G A B C

One Octave

Tones and semitones

If you count all the notes (including black keys) in an octave, you will get 12, making up the octave's 12 semitones. Notes that are adjacent to one another are a semitone apart. The distance between two notes separated by one note is a whole tone; thus two semitones form a whole tone. Since there are only seven note names (A–G) for the white notes, various signs had to be developed to include all the other notes within the octave. These signs are called accidentals.

Accidentals

These are the signs that alter the pitch of a note when written before it. A sharp sign (♯) raises a note by one semitone. A flat (♭) lowers a note by one semitone. Accidentals only apply to subsequent notes in the same bar. Thus if a G is sharpened (♯) – the middle black note of the group of three – all subsequent Gs in the same bar are sharpened. A bar line cancels all accidentals that occur in the previous bar. If a sharp or flat in the same bar is cancelled, a natural sign ( ) is used. That is, all notes are in their 'natural' state unless flattened or sharpened; a natural sign is not written out for each one.

Key signature

A key signature is a collection of sharps or flats at the beginning of a piece of music denoting that all subsequent notes on that pitch are altered. Thus, if an F-sharp occurs at the beginning of the piece as a key signature, all Fs in the piece are sharpened unless a natural sign alters them. Bear in mind that this natural sign would only alter subsequent notes in the same bar, the bar line once again enforcing the key signature.

There is an order in which sharps and flats are introduced into a key signature. The first sharp is always F-sharp, the next one, C-sharp. Thus, if a piece has a key signature of one sharp it is always F-sharp. If it has two sharps it is always F-sharp and C-sharp. The full order is F, C, G, D, A, E and B. The order in which flats are introduced into a key signature is exactly the other way around (B, E, A, D, G, C, F).

TONES AND SEMITONES

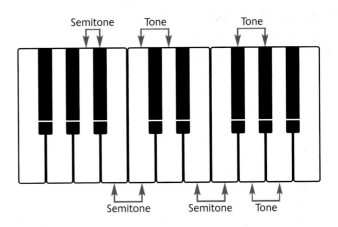

ACCIDENTALS

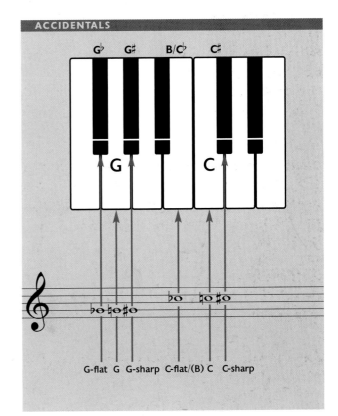

KEY SIGNATURE

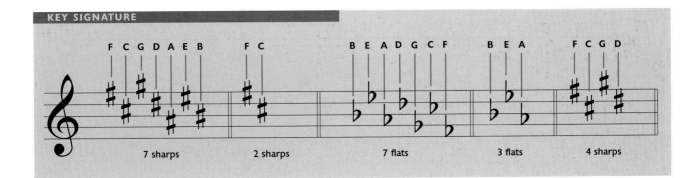

TRANSPOSING INSTRUMENTS

If you were to play a C on the clarinet and a C on the piano, you'd soon realize you're not hearing the same note. This is because all modern clarinets and saxophones are transposing instruments – the pitch of the notes sounds higher or lower than written. Also, since not all the instruments are equal in size, the pitch they produce with the same fingering will differ. This generally means that each different-sized clarinet and saxophone would have to have a different fingering, which would make it very difficult for a saxophonist to switch from a tenor to an alto (see below), for example. So a ruling was established that the fingering be kept consistent and the pitch of the written notations simply be moved up or down.

Take a clarinet in B-flat as an example: it sounds a whole tone – or major second – lower than the written notation. If you played a C on the B-flat clarinet, it would sound like a B-flat on the piano (hence the naming of the clarinet after this pitch). So, if you write the part for the B-flat clarinet a whole tone higher, you would get the note you are looking for. Thus, if you wanted to produce the sound of a concert pitch A (the note an orchestra uses to tune their instruments), you would play a B – a major second higher – on the B-flat clarinet.

This concept takes some time to figure out and most music students struggle with it for years. Do not feel ashamed if you don't understand after the first reading.

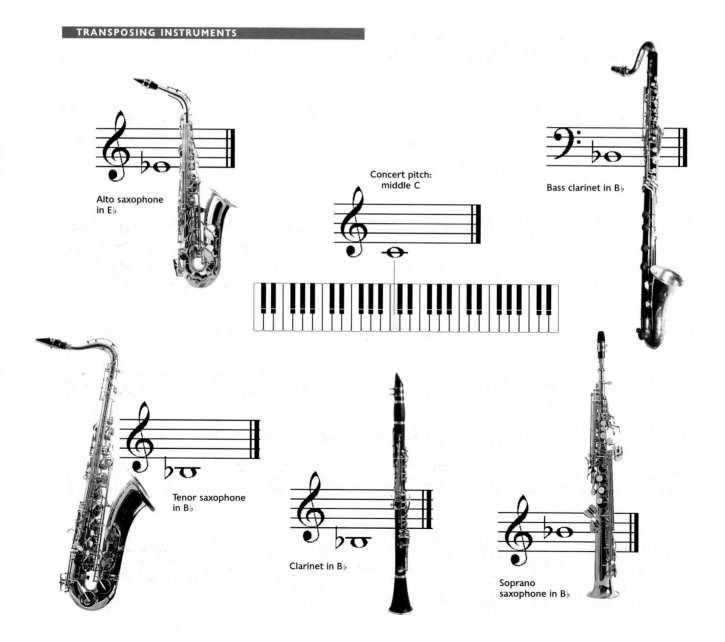

TRANSPOSING INSTRUMENTS

Alto saxophone in E♭

Concert pitch: middle C

Bass clarinet in B♭

Tenor saxophone in B♭

Clarinet in B♭

Soprano saxophone in B♭

TRANSPOSING INSTRUMENTS

Concert pitch: These are the notes that we wish to hear. Semitones are marked with a slur (curved line).

E-flat clarinet & alto saxophone: Sounds three semitones higher and is therefore written three semitones lower.

B-flat clarinet & tenor saxophone: Sounds two semitones lower and is therefore written two semitones higher.

A-clarinet: Sounds three semitones lower and is therefore written three semitones higher.

B-flat bass clarinet: Sounds 14 semitones (an octave plus two semitones) lower and is therefore written 10 semitones (an octave minus two semitones) lower.

Pitch exercises

That should be enough theory to get you started. Now try the following exercises to read the pitch. The rhythm of all the notes is equal so that you do not have to concentrate overmuch on this aspect.

Since you do not know how to play these notes yet (which are explained in the fingering charts on pages 36–7), simply recognize the name of the note for now. Also make sure that you know when a bar line enforces the key signature.

PITCH EXERCISES

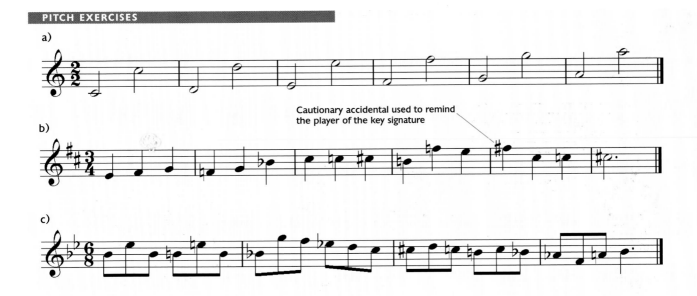

Cautionary accidental used to remind the player of the key signature

chapter three

HOW DO I PLAY?

IF TWO CLARINETTISTS WERE TO PLAY an identical piece on an identical instrument — and they were taught by the same teacher and made use of the same playing technique — their respective sounds would still be different. No two players or instruments sound the same, and it is quite easy to understand why. The instruments might be of a different make; different mouthpieces will also greatly affect their respective sound. Differences between the players are subtle and less easy to distinguish. They might have different breathing techniques, different fingering or tonguing techniques, not to mention different musical natures. One's own distinctive way of playing is usually an outflow of diverging teaching techniques by various teachers. One teacher may demand one thing, while another will refuse to allow it in her class! In this respect, there are as many techniques of playing the clarinet and saxophone as there are teachers to teach them — and even though a musician's playing technique might remain roughly consistent with other players, he will find his own personal way of producing the sound that pleases him most. This chapter aims to list in a logical order the faculties a player must possess and develop for playing the clarinet and saxophone.

The many opinions on what constitutes the 'correct' way of playing can lead to heated arguments and mutual antagonism between players and teachers. While it may be very entertaining to watch, taking sides will not get you anywhere; simply be aware that these differing opinions do exist. If you pick up another book on saxophone or clarinet technique, you may discover aspects that differ greatly from this book. In the end, the only 'correct' technique is your own. You will know intuitively (after a few years) what works for you and what does not. Therefore, read as many books and assimilate as many opinions as you can; they will all lead you to a refined technique that suits you perfectly.

Another thing to consider is technique as a musical tool. Somebody with an outstanding technique will be capable of playing pieces that require superhuman ability, but even though the public enjoys this display of showmanship, there is just as much merit in being able to play an easy piece beautifully. It's no use making music simply for showmanship's sake (although the money is better!), especially if the piece is so difficult that you end up playing it badly.

OPPOSITE Although it is difficult to discipline yourself to practise regularly, you should not shy away from this, as it is the key to becoming a good player.

ASSEMBLING YOUR INSTRUMENT

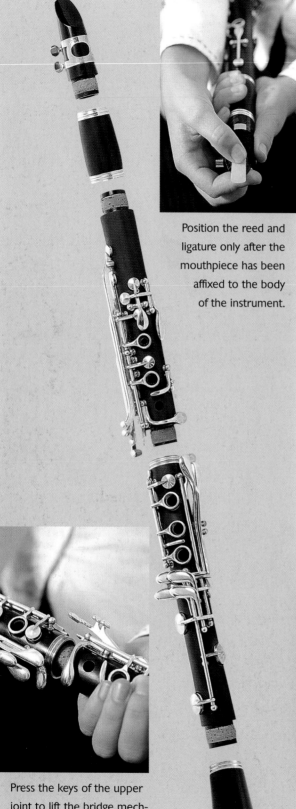

Position the reed and ligature only after the mouthpiece has been affixed to the body of the instrument.

Press the keys of the upper joint to lift the bridge mechanism prior to assembly.

When you open the case of a clarinet or saxophone, you will immediately notice that the instrument is not assembled. This is a means of saving space. Before you even attempt to start playing, it is essential to be able to assemble your instrument.

- Take notice of how the various parts are packed in the cavities of the case. Trying to force parts into incorrect cavities could damage the key mechanism.
- For the same reason, do not lift any parts of the instrument out of the case by the key mechanism.

Clarinet
- When assembling a clarinet, start by rubbing special cork grease on the joints between the different parts of the instrument. This decreases friction when assembling the joints and makes the cork last longer. It also helps to effect an airtight seal between the various joints of the instrument.
- Firstly, connect the bell and lower joint using a twisting motion.
- Now that the lower part of the instrument is assembled, add the upper joint. It is important to keep the keys of the upper joint depressed, thereby lifting the bridge mechanism, to avoid damaging it when the two parts are twisted together. Resting the bell on your knee will give added support.
- Now, twist on the barrel, keeping a firm grip with your fingers on the keys (not the key mechanism) of the upper joint.

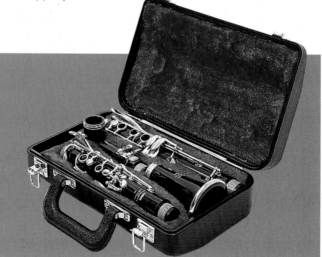

ABOVE Ensure that you're well versed in which part of the instrument fits into which cavity of the case to avoid damaging the key mechanism.

Saxophone

- When assembling a saxophone, rub cork grease on the joint between the neck and the body. Even though this joint usually only consists of metal, the grease will preserve the joint and also make assembly easier, especially if the instrument is still cold. Then tighten the screw.
- Finish off by placing the mouthpiece on the instrument.

Assembling the mouthpiece

Clarinet and Saxophone

- Start off by moistening the reed — a moist reed vibrates more easily than a dry one and gives a more stable tone. This can be done by placing the reed in lukewarm water a minute before starting to play. Other players suck on the reed for half a minute, using their saliva to moisten it.
- Place the loosened ligature on the mouthpiece. Which way the screws face is up to you, but most players tend to have the screws on the underside where the reed is.
- Place the moistened reed on the mouthpiece under the ligature and make sure that the tip and sides of the reed are in line with the tip and rails of the mouthpiece.
- End the procedure by sliding the loosened ligature into place and then tightening the screws.
- Test the reed by blowing a few notes. If it feels very hard to play or does not respond very well, try moving the ligature down a bit. It is important to experiment with the reed's position to find out what suits your playing best.

Applying cork grease is not only beneficial to the joints of an instrument, but also makes assembling the instrument easier.

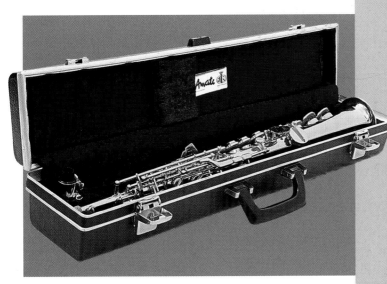

ABOVE Most instrument cases have extra cavities to store reeds, cork grease, neck straps, extra mouthpieces and cleaning gear.

Packing your instrument away

After you have finished playing, it is essential to disassemble your instrument and pack it away. There are many reasons for doing so, but the most important is to prolong the life of your instrument.

- Start by separating all the joints in the opposite sequence that you put them together. Remember to depress the keys on the upper joint of the clarinet when separating it from the lower joint to ensure the safety of the bridge mechanism.
- Clean the grease off the joints using a clean, dry cloth or tissue paper. Just rub lightly in order to remove the excess grease, but try to leave a thin film of it on the cork since this keeps the cork in good shape.
- Use the swab or a cloth attached to a weight and drag the cloth two or three times through the various parts of the instrument. This removes the moisture caused by playing. It will prevent wooden instruments from cracking and metal instruments from warping. It also ensures that no horrible smell greets your nostrils the next time you play.
- Wiping the keys with a soft dry cloth will remove any oil left behind from your fingers, which could discolour them.
- Loosen the ligature and remove the reed from the mouthpiece. Rinse the reed and dry it off with a cloth.
- Thoroughly dry the mouthpiece. If you have a reed guard, place the reed in it; if you don't, put the reed back on the mouthpiece and move it backward before tightening the screws on the ligature, then put a guard over the mouthpiece.
- Pack the various parts of the instrument in their corresponding cavities in the case. Remember to handle the various parts in such a way that you do not damage the key mechanism.

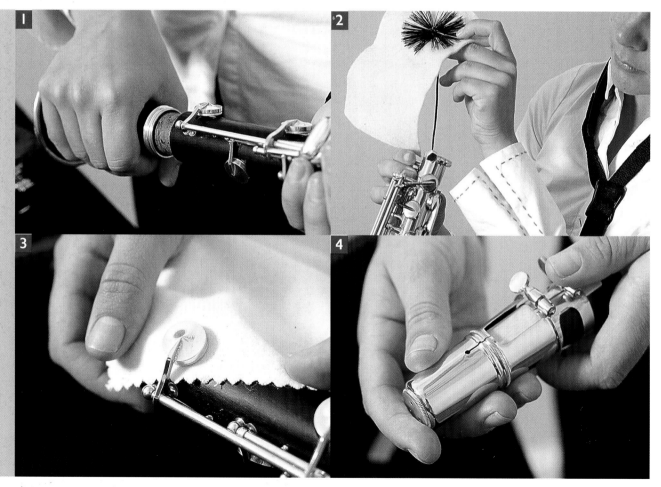

1) Start by carefully disassembling the instrument.
2) Use a weighted cloth to dry the condensation inside the body of the instrument.
3) A cloth placed between body and keypads prolongs pad life.
4) If you do not have reed guards, place the reed back on the mouthpiece after cleaning.

POSTURE

Your posture should be such that it allows you to breathe freely and that you're comfortable and relaxed. The posture for playing the clarinet or saxophone is mostly concerned with the upper body, since the lower body will either be sitting (orchestra) or standing, and even walking (marching band). The upper body should be upright, but not rigid, shoulders straight and relaxed, head tilted slightly downward. With clarinets and straight soprano saxophones, the instrument is held straight, in front of you. Alto, tenor, baritone and bass saxophones are held at an angle. When sitting, the body and bell of the instrument rests against your right leg. When standing or walking, it rests against your right hip. Tilt your head slightly to the left to accommodate the angle of the neck and mouthpiece of the instrument.

Breathing

Breath should, whenever possible, be drawn in through the mouth since it is possible to breathe more air in a shorter amount of time through the mouth than through the nose. If you watch a baby breathing, you will notice that the stomach moves and not the chest as it does with adults. This 'natural', abdominal breathing pushes out the stomach; more space is created for the intestines, which lowers the diaphragm and causes a vacuum for the lungs to expand into. Breathing through the mouth, at the same time expanding your stomach, is the surest way to fill your lungs with lots of fresh air.

Once your chest is filled with air, you can start to produce notes on the instrument. This means releasing your supply of air into the mouthpiece in order to get the reed to vibrate, thereby producing the notes. The most important thing to remember is not to release all your air at once (think of your air supply as money in a bank account – spending it all at the beginning of the month will definitely cause problems later on!). The airflow has to be controlled. This is done mainly by your diaphragm – the membrane dividing the cavity of your upper body into two halves: the lower part contains your intestines, the top part your lungs, heart, pancreas, and so on. Imitating the action required to do a sit-up while standing will tell you where it is; this is called activating the diaphragm. For soft notes the diaphragm has to work quite hard to control the flow of air, while the opposite is the case with loud notes.

RIGHT Curved saxophones rest on the right hip (standing) or thigh (sitting), while straight instruments like the clarinet or soprano saxophone are held straight in front of the player.

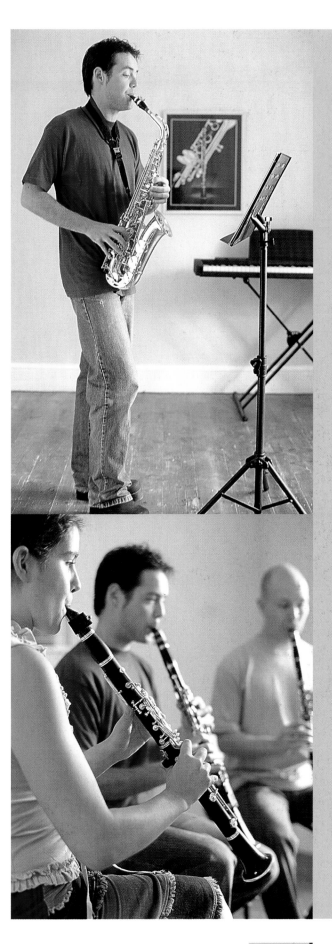

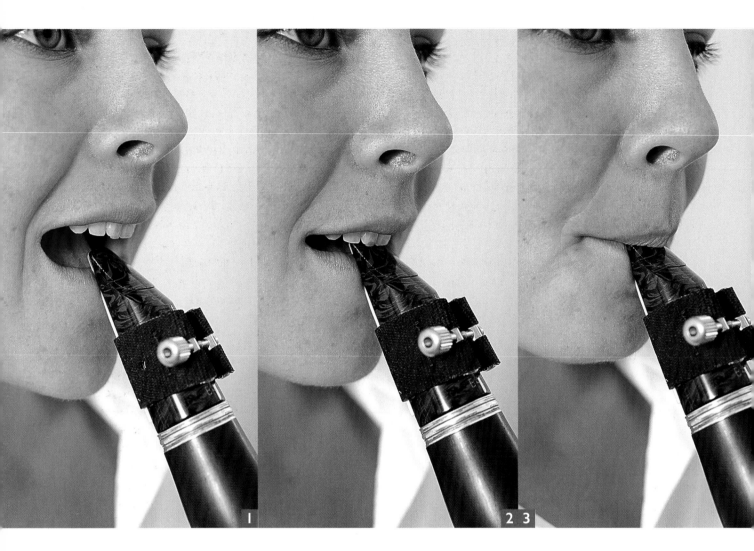

Embouchure

Embouchure is a grand word that refers to the placement and working of the tongue, teeth, mouth and various facial muscles around the mouthpiece in order to control the movement of the reed and thereby the sound produced. The embouchure for the clarinet and saxophone are roughly the same, which explains why especially jazz musicians do not have a problem switching between them. As a general rule, the embouchure becomes more relaxed the bigger the instrument gets. However, you will have to adjust it on every instrument you play until you find a way that suits your playing best. Therefore the following points should only serve as a guideline for embouchure on the clarinet and saxophone:

- Begin by pushing your lower lip over your lower teeth with your fingers. Once you are used to the feeling, repeat this action using the mouthpiece instead. The reed should now be in contact with your lower lip, keeping it in place over the lower teeth.

- Next, lower your upper teeth onto the top of the mouthpiece. You should avoid biting it since this will put too much pressure on the reed and lessen your control over it; simply rest your teeth on the mouthpiece.

- Lower your upper lip over your upper teeth, bringing it into contact with the mouthpiece.

- Now start blowing, using your facial muscles around your mouth to keep your lips firmly in place so that no air escapes. No breath should escape from your mouth – your entire air supply should flow through the instrument. Do not relax your cheeks or allow them to puff outwards.

ABOVE, LEFT TO RIGHT 1) Start by curving your bottom lip over your lower teeth, then gently rest the mouthpiece against the lower lip.

2) Lower the upper teeth onto the mouthpiece; don't bite.
3) Lower the upper lip over the upper teeth to form a seal and then start blowing.

Tonguing

Tonguing refers to stopping the vibrations of the reed with the tip of your tongue. Saying 'tu-tu-tu' can mimic the movement of the tongue. There are many different kinds of tonguing: legato (tied) tonguing, which is the normal way of tonguing as described on p27; staccato (short) tonguing, where the tongue flicks the reed quickly; soft tonguing (where the movement of the tongue is lazy); and hard tonguing (where the movement is sharp and decisive). Remember that the different signs in musical notation indicate which type of tonguing should be used (see p27); this is called articulation.

- If there are no slurs or other articulation markings, normal legato tonguing is used.
- A staccato note is produced using staccato tonguing (no surprise there!).
- Loud or accented notes are produced using hard tonguing while soft notes or notes with a tenuto above them are made using soft tonguing.

Fingering

Fingering refers to the manipulation of the key mechanism by the fingers, thereby influencing the length of the vibrating column of air within the instrument, and in turn raising or lowering the pitch produced. The most important thing to remember is that the further the fingers are from the keys, the more time they will need to travel the distance to each one.

Thus, it is desirable to keep your fingers close to the keys at all times and not to have them sticking out at all angles. Simply allow the fingers to rest just above the keys and depress the finger(s) needed for a specific note, leaving your other fingers in their state of 'rest'. This is a lot more difficult than it sounds as you will soon realize that your fingers do not always obey your brain's commands. Luckily, this improves with time and can be practised, so there is no need to worry excessively.

Fingering charts have been included on pp36–37 for most of the written notes for clarinet and saxophone. In the beginning you will refer to them often, but as time passes it should become second nature to connect the written note with the correct fingering. The very high and low notes are difficult to play, but some of these notes have been given so that you are aware of their existence.

One important tip concerning fingering: all the keys on the saxophone are connected to pads that close the tone holes, therefore you only have to depress a key to effect the relevant seal. Some of the keys on the clarinet, however, are open and require you to close them only with the fingers. If they are not closed completely, the notes will not sound properly or will sound out of tune (or not sound at all). Another difficult fingering on the clarinet involves the speaker key (the key labelled (a) on the illustration on p37). It needs to be depressed by the top half of the thumb, while the lower half needs to close the hole below it.

Hand positions for clarinet: left hand (1) and right hand (2); and for sax: left hand (3) and right hand (4).

FINGERING CHARTS

Saxophone

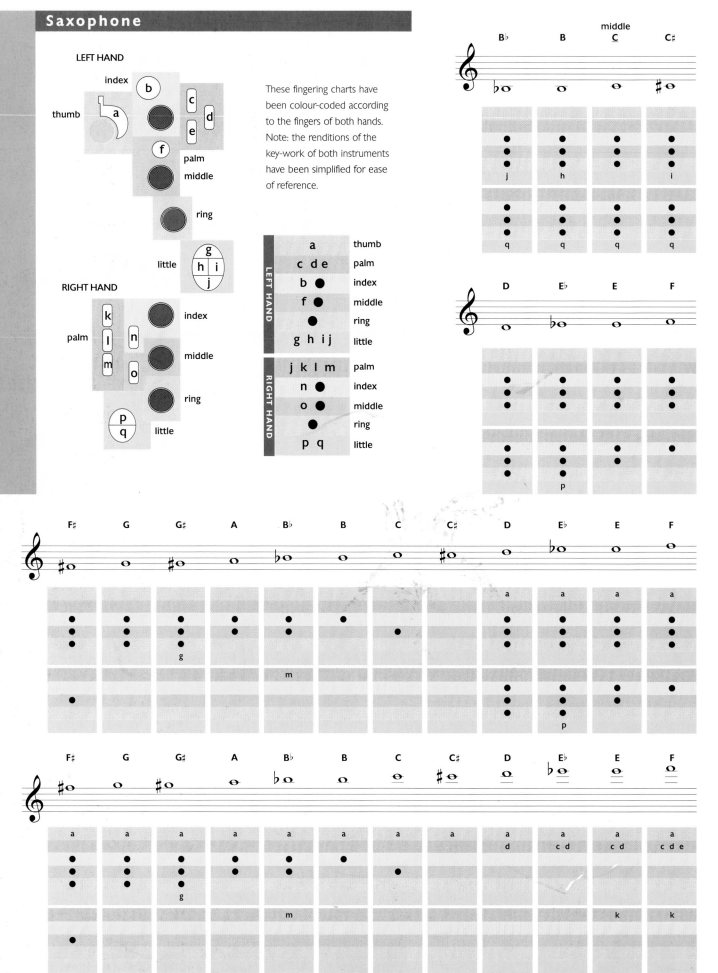

These fingering charts have been colour-coded according to the fingers of both hands. Note: the renditions of the key-work of both instruments have been simplified for ease of reference.

Clarinet

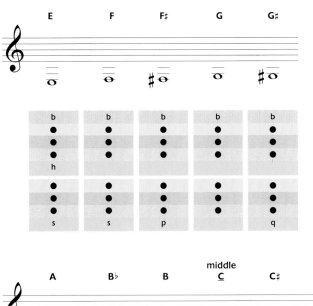

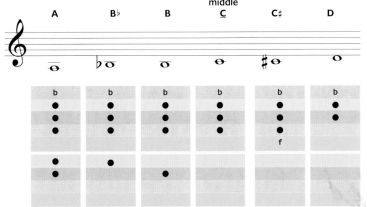

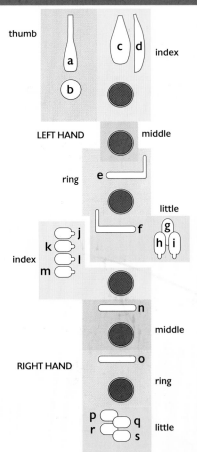

Not all different makes of instruments have the same number of keys, but the differences are usually restricted to one or two additional keys. These are also usually keys that are seldom used.

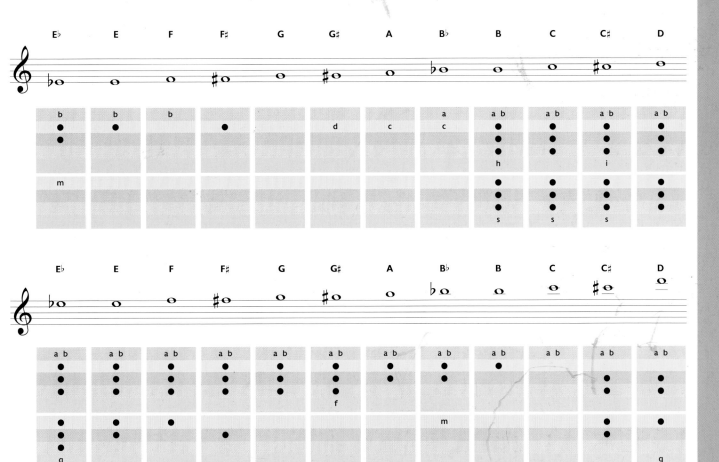

WHY PRACTISE TECHNICAL EXERCISES?

All the previously mentioned aspects of playing the clarinet or saxophone are collectively referred to as your technique. A musician with a good technique is respected by his or her peers and can usually play anything that you can throw at him or her. It is therefore essential to develop this technique should you wish to make progress in your playing and especially if you wish to play with other musicians. To this end there are many technical exercises that help to promote certain aspects of technique; a few exercises have been included in this book to cover some of these.

Each instrument has some problems that are intimately bound to its construction, and these technical exercises are meant to help the player overcome them. However, the repetitive practice of technical exercises can become boring, so it's important to do these exercises only if you really wish to develop technique. They should not be used as an end in themselves — lest you stop playing out of sheer boredom. As soon as they start to bore you, move on to something more interesting. It would be a pity, however, not to make use of them as the rewards are usually worth it.

Constant practice can become monotonous, but it really is the only way to achieve good playing technique.

Exercise 1 — Breathing

The first important technique that will have to be practised is how to breathe correctly. The basic procedure has been explained on p33, but there are many different exercises that will help you to develop 'correct' breathing habits. There are many added advantages to doing these exercises, apart from developing your technique. Taking deep steadying breaths not only lowers your heart rate, but also increases your lung capacity and increases the oxygen content in your blood-stream. Playing a wind instrument is therefore beneficial to anybody who likes sport or who leads an active lifestyle. Start by simply taking a deep breath (but not too deep) and holding it in. After a slow count of 10, start to release the air supply slowly, blowing out through the mouth while making an

'f' sound. Make sure that you do not expend half of your breath supply right at the beginning (or the 'attack' as it is often called), but that you control the slow release of air, using your diaphragm and larynx (the back of your throat). Repeat this exercise a few times a day, away from the instrument. Also be certain to take breaks in-between otherwise you might hyperventilate. Now you can take up your instrument and repeat the procedure. Try to produce a stable note without any fluctuations in tone, timbre (tone colour) or dynamics (intensity) for as long as possible. It is important to do this exercise on one note only. After you have done this, repeat the note, but stop the airflow periodically when blowing out. This is another excellent way to practise breath control.

Exercise 2 — Tonguing

This exercise is to help the tongue become more agile — remember that tonguing concerns the brief stopping of the reed by the tongue. This exercise should be practised slowly (especially in the beginning), but can be gradually sped up as you progress. Start with normal tonguing, then staccato tonguing and then soft and hard tonguing. Experiment with the different types of tonguing and learn to become aware of the exact movement that the tongue makes.

Exercise 3 — Dynamics

This exercise is much the same as the first one, but in this one you must gradually change the dynamics of the note you play. As the note's intensity changes, it affects the vibration of the reed. It's therefore important to adapt your embouchure to accommodate this change.

Trying to play the same note both loudly and softly with the same embouchure is not really possible since the intensity of the airflow is also vastly different. Remember that the diaphragm has to work harder the softer you play. One very important aspect that will help to make practising technical exercises more enjoyable is variation. Although practice is often repetitive, varying the way in which you practise will keep you focused for longer. Experiment with the speed when you change from one dynamic level to another, to vary this exercise. See how fast or how slow you can go from *piano* to *forte*.

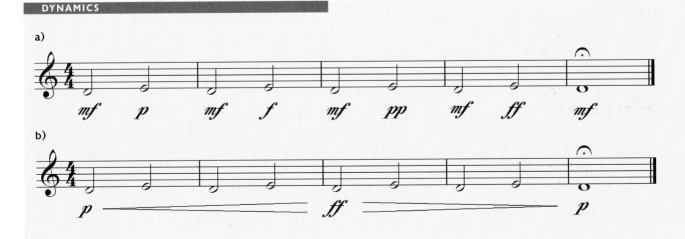

Exercise 4 — Articulation

This exercise is designed to be very confusing at first. It must help the eye convert articulation signs directly into the appropriate movements of the tongue.

Start this exercise slowly and gradually speed it up. You are likely to feel extremely bewildered in the beginning, but this skill also develops over time. Before you know it you will articulate music correctly without even having to think about it on a conscious level. If you do become confused, make sure you go back and revise the section on articulation in Chapter 2 (p27).

ARTICULATION

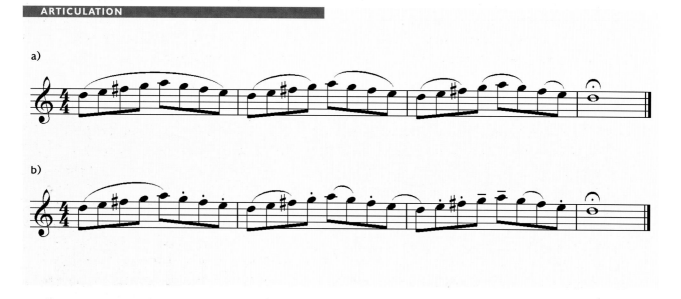

Exercise 5 — Intervals

Playing different notes legato (without tonguing) involves more than just changing your fingering. The lengthening and shortening of the air column also affects the vibrations of the reed. If you do not adjust your embouchure to accommodate the new pitch, you will find that the instrument (especially the clarinet) squeaks or makes other undesirable noises. As your technique progresses, your embouchure will automatically adjust to accommodate a new note. In the meantime, this exercise is good for helping you develop this aspect.

Also remember that it is extremely important, especially in the beginning, to take regular breaks when practising. Constant playing can be very tiring and you will not be able to enjoy your hobby if you suffer a concussion because of hyperventilation!

INTERVALS

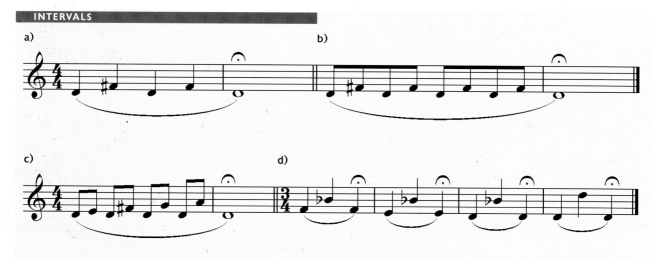

HOW TO PRACTISE A PIECE

Now that you have become acquainted with the technical aspects of playing, we can move on to playing an actual piece of music. Therefore, an array of pieces has been added in the following chapter for your enjoyment. You must remember, however, that it is unlikely that you will be able to play a piece perfectly the first time. This is why most musicians have to practise a piece before they play it to an audience. Practising in a systematic way will decrease the amount of time it takes to learn a new piece and will also teach you how to practise effectively. Here are some tips that should help you achieve results faster than you would if you went about it in a disorderly and unsystematic way. It must, however, be said that practising should never become an end in itself lest optimism turns into pessimism. Therefore, follow these tips as far as you are able, but never forget that the reason why you're doing this is to make music. You must have fun.

- Start by making sure that you know how to finger (which keys to depress) all the notes in the piece. In the beginning this will be a tedious affair and you will have to refer to the fingering chart (page 36–7) quite often. As time progresses, however, you will automatically know the correct fingering for a note. This is why it is important to read a lot of music often.
- Play each note individually, as explained in exercise 1. Also tongue each note individually so that you can become used to the position of your tongue and embouchure.
- Now practise the intervals between adjacent notes, like in exercise 5. This will help you to become adept at adjusting your embouchure to accommodate the new note. If the adjacent notes go over the break of the clarinet (A on the second space to B on the third line), this is especially difficult and it is very important that you practise it.
- Practise slowly. Once your fingers and notes are secure, you can speed up your playing gradually. You are not going to impress anybody if you can play a piece at the speed of light but in a slovenly way.
- Divide the piece into sections and concentrate on one section at a time. It is often difficult to focus on a piece in its entirety and this will help you to remain focused.
- When you make a mistake, never simply ignore it and play on. Stop and play the section again. You should play it perfectly at least five times before you continue to the next section.
- Try not to look at your hands too often. Your hands should learn to be intuitive in feeling out the right keys and fingering.

- Even if you are good at memorizing the music, it is important that you play with the music in front of you. A person who relies on memorization too much (although it does have its place) usually has poor sight-reading, and that inhibits him from learning new pieces.
- Make sure that you keep a constant beat. Even if a piece has a very free tempo, you should play the notes 'straight' (exactly as written) when you practise a new piece for the first time. You can keep time by lightly tapping your foot. If you want something else to count out the beats for you, invest in a metronome. These are mechanical or electronic devices with an adjustable beat. They tend to make your playing sound a little robotic, but it's very important to be able to maintain a steady beat, especially if you are playing with other musicians.

ABOVE AND RIGHT Metronomes come in various shapes and sizes, including mechanical, electronic and digital.

chapter four

KNOW YOUR MUSIC

WHY WOULD ANYONE WANT TO LEARN ABOUT the history of a piece of music or its composer? It is important to realize that no music (or any other work of art, for that matter) is created in a vacuum. There is always a specific reason or context that causes a piece of music to come into being. In this sense, music is always written with a particular audience in mind, to fill a specific function, or to express the emotions of the composer. This information might be of passing interest only to a person who merely wants to listen to a piece of music (see Chapter 5), but it is absolutely essential for a person who wishes to play it. It is, of course, quite possible to play a piece by Mozart without knowing who he was, when he lived and for whom he wrote, but this lends a certain 'flatness' to your understanding of the composer and his music. The study of music history is a fascinating subject that can become a hobby all on its own. Nevertheless, if you are not interested in history, it is still important to know something as it helps form your interpretation of a piece. Musical interpretation is a wonderfully varied and complex thing. The older music is, the less certainty we have concerning the composers' intentions. This is why especially 'classical' music has such lasting appeal. Each generation of players has a new take on the matter, which causes the way in which we hear Bach or Beethoven to constantly evolve.

Musical interpretation can be broken down into three levels. The first concerns an accurate rendition of the little black notes on the paper and the composer's various interpretive markings (see p26). Secondly, knowing the historical context and performance practices of a given era or milieu will help you to understand the intent of the composer at a deeper level (which, in essence, is what most musical performers hope to achieve). Lastly, interpretation is a set of highly personal parameters such as your own taste and musical sensibilities, as a result of which no two musicians' interpretations of the same piece will sound exactly the same. It is this kind of wondrous variety that makes music such a living, dynamic art form. This applies equally to 'popular' music. The version of a song you hear on a CD will not sound the same as the live performance or the 'unplugged' concert.

This chapter introduces you to some of the historical eras in which music was created and gives suggestions on the first and second levels of interpretation.

OPPOSITE Playing composers of the past establishes a link with those great artistic minds.

Learning a piece of music

In the previous chapter, you learned various techniques to help you to practise a piece of music effectively and systematically. In this chapter, which contains a selection of pieces spanning approximately 300 years, the idea is to give the reader (player) some insight into how one goes about interpreting music. This includes explanations of both the first and second levels of interpretation (the third cannot really be learned from books). The first will be discussed in each separate piece under the heading of Playing Notes, while the second is explained by a brief discussion of the various centuries in which the relevant composers wrote their music. One thing that the reader must bear in mind is that most of these pieces were not originally written for clarinet or saxophone, but are arrangements. The reason for this is simply that most pieces written for a beginner on these instruments

are usually excessively boring and nothing special, musically. 'Good' music, written specifically for clarinet and saxophone, was written by composers who had a specific virtuoso in mind, and therefore such pieces are usually extremely difficult and quite impossible for the beginner. This is a common problem and most musicians agree that arrangements are a good way of introducing a beginner to music that is worthwhile and easy enough to play.

NOTE: The pieces have all been transcribed for a B-flat instrument (as B-flat clarinets are the most common kind of clarinet in use). Thus, a B-flat clarinet, and soprano and tenor sax are able to play these pieces with the accompaniment. If you play the alto saxophone in E-flat or the clarinet in A- or E-flat, the accompaniment will have to be transposed. A good accompanist should be able to do this on sight.

PLAYING NOTES

- Look firstly at the top right-hand corner. Check who the composer is. It is important to orientate yourself from the start to the style of the music. In this case it is Wolfgang Amadeus Mozart, a late-18th-century Austrian composer.
- Often, an opus or work number will be at the top of the page. It specifies the exact work and often gives a clue as to when it was written – in most cases the smaller the opus number, the earlier the work. The works of Mozart are catalogued by KV (Köchel Verzeichnis) or just K.
- Look at the name of the piece and see if it gives any clues as to its interpretation. This piece is the theme of a set of variations originally written for piano; the theme of a set of variations is usually played quite slowly to give the listener a clear idea of the theme and its harmonies so that he can recognize their permutations in the variations.
- Look at the tempo marking in the top left-hand corner so that you know how fast or slow the piece should be played. This piece has no tempo indication, but bearing in mind the previous point, Andante (at a moderate pace) would be a good tempo.
- Look at the time signature. Check if it remains constant throughout. In this piece of music it does.
- Look at the key signature. Are there any changes throughout the piece? In this case the key signature has three sharps: F, C, and G – there are no changes in the key signature throughout the piece.

Theme and Variations

KV 454a

Wolfgang Amadeus Mozart

Theme

- Scan the piece for accidentals. Obviously, they will indicate any notes that differ from the key signature.
- Look at the dynamic markings. If the melodic line and accompaniment are on the same page, the dynamic markings will be written between the melody and the accompaniment. If the dynamics of the melody differ from the accompaniment, another set of markings will appear between the two staves of the accompaniment (also called the grand stave). In this piece there are no dynamic markings. However, convention dictates that the repeat of a section will differ in dynamics (it is usually softer when played for the second time).
- Scan the piece for articulation signs like slurs, accents, staccato's, etc. This will give you indications of where you can breathe. Mark your breathing points on the page. A tick ✔ will suffice and is used in this book to indicate a place to breathe.
- Lastly, make sure you understand the meanings of all other interpretive markings and words that you come across.

THE 17TH CENTURY

A question that often arises is why one would wish to play or study music from this particular century, when the clarinet only developed in the following one and the saxophone in the century after that.

The answer lies in the fact that it is not possible to build a house without a foundation. The reason why we study and play the music from the 17th century is because it was in this time that the foundations of all later instrumental compositions were laid. This is the time in which the concerto (see p77) and the sonata (see p79) developed and when purely instrumental compositions became another vehicle by which a composer could pursue his craft. It does not mean that instrumental music did not exist before this time; on the contrary. Instruments formed an integral part of European musical life before the 17th century. The church, which until then was the centre of European culture, preferred purely vocal compositions, however, so most instrumental music could only be heard at court or among the peasants. Unfortunately, relatively few of these compositions have survived since literacy was largely restricted to clerical circles.

Historians often write that the 17th century saw the emancipation of instrumental music (also referred to as the Baroque period). This is due to two main factors, namely, the growth of aristocratic influence and the rapid development in instrument building. Despite the fact that the European

The growing popularity of wind instruments was even reflected in French faïence work of the day.

In the lavish courts of the changing new aristocracy, the early form of orchestra played itself out in opulent opera houses.

aristocracy had been around since the Middle Ages, the church had always had the most political clout. In the 15th and 16th centuries, Europe began to secularize with the renewed interest in humanistic concepts and ideologies, and in the 17th century, courts like that of Louis XIV in France, were established, becoming models of such extravagant elegance and opulence that most courts wished to emulate them. It is in this competitive environment that instrumental music was allowed to flourish.

Two classes of instruments that were especially important in this regard were keyboard instruments (like the organ, harpsichord and clavichord) and the violin family. Without the restriction of words, composers were permitted to give flight to their fancies, and the instrumental music of this time made use of certain devices to illustrate certain moods. Crashing chords could signal a thunderstorm while drooping melodies would signal anything from death to depression. These 'affectations' became so systematic that their mere presence would alert the listener to the intention of the composer.

Another important musical development was the polarization of melody and bass line. In the previous centuries, vocal polyphony (multi-voiced writing) dictated that all voices were equally important, whereas now the inner voices were marginalized to give greater prominence to the melody and bass. This was caused, in part, by the development and popularity of opera early in the 17th century, where melody was considered the most fundamental aspect of the music (the early divas of the stage were not interested in singing music that did not give them sufficient scope to perform one set of vocal acrobatics after the other). One very important thing to remember when playing music from this century is that composers were not the emancipated artistic individuals we think of today. Composers, who were not afforded any great respect, were treated just like any other servants – and they performed their musical duties when they were required to by their employers. A composer who lived in this era was employed by the church, court or the local town council and had relatively little freedom to write music to suit his own artistic ends, but had to write music to satisfy the political and artistic agendas of his employer. A perfect example is the composer Heinrich Schütz (1585–1672). When the finances of his patrons allowed it, he would write large-scale works for orchestra, choir and soloists. When war started to drain the finances, he was reduced to writing for one singer with keyboard accompaniment. Though this appears to be a precarious situation, we must remember that the socio-political surroundings of a

composer always influences his musical output. Another good example of this phenomenon is Johann Sebastian Bach (1685–1750). Despite the fact that he lived in an age when opera was considered all the rage throughout Europe, he did not write a single one. This was not because he disliked the genre, but simply because he never worked for anybody who had a theatre. Even though composers had limited opportunities in this regard, some of them did such a good job that we have been left with works of art that have weathered centuries. That is what makes it worth taking the time to actually get to know and play music from this time.

ABOVE Like most composers of the age, German music-writer Heinrich Schütz had to write music that suited the artistic agendas of his employers.

SOME FAMOUS COMPOSERS

1567–1643	Claudio Monteverdi
1585–1672	Heinrich Schütz
1632–1687	Jean-Baptiste Lully
1637–1707	Dietrich Buxtehude
1643–1704	Marc-Antoine Charpentier
1649–1708	John Blow
1653–1713	Arcangelo Corelli
1658–1695	Henry Purcell
1660–1725	Alessandro Scarlatti
1668–1733	Francois Couperin
1678–1741	Antonio Vivaldi
1681–1767	Georg Philipp Telemann
1683–1729	Johann David Heinichen
1683–1764	Jean-Philippe Rameau
1685–1750	Johann Sebastian Bach

PLAYING NOTES

- Composers were not always very specific when indicating the dynamics of a piece. The most one can hope for is an indication of loud or soft, but no gradual change from the one to the other. Changing abruptly from one dynamic level to another, which is called 'terraced' dynamics, is usually applied to sections that are repeated.

- Melodies are often embellished by the use of ornaments. This includes trills (a rapid alteration between two adjacent notes) and various other signs which alter the melody. Ornaments are often indicated in the music, but they are most often improvised.

- Improvisation, which literally means making something up on the spot, is an important feature of the music from this time, but it requires a lot of specialized knowledge and should be done with discretion.

47

Jean-Philippe Rameau

Rameau was born in Dijon to a father who was an organist and a mother who was of the lesser nobility. He was the seventh of 11 surviving children and learnt from his father to 'read music before he could even read'. We know very little about the first 40 years of his life because he was very secretive about this period in later life. He might have made a short stay in Italy, where he picked up his preference for opera. He held various posts as organist in the provinces, but the musical cosmopolitanism of Paris was calling him to greater exploits. The story goes that, after failing to obtain his release from a post at Clermont, he proceeded to play so horrendously during a service that his employers were happy to get rid of him.

Soon after his move to Paris, he published his treatise on harmony and music theory. It was such a hit that he became famous overnight and it has remained one of the seminal works of music theory till this day. He is also well known as a composer of operas, cantatas (see p79) and various pieces for keyboard like 'Les Sauvages' (which he wrote after attending a performance by two Louisiana Indians).

Jean-Philippe Rameau
1683–1764

PLAYING NOTES

- The title says that this piece is a minuet in the form of a rondeau (rondo). The minuet is a stately dance at a moderate tempo with three beats to the bar. Rondo-form can be summarized as ABA, with A being the first section and B the second section. The first section ends at the double bar line. The second section goes to the end of the piece. The da capo at the end means that you have to repeat from the beginning until the fine, which means that you end at that point – ABA.

- There is no tempo indication (as is often the case in early music), but it should not be played too fast since the minuet is not a lively dance.

- The time signature indicates that there are three quarter note beats to a bar.

- Remember to ignore the key signature of the accompaniment and focus on the clarinet part, which has no flats or sharps.

- There are no dynamic markings (as is also often the case with early music), but since each section can be divided into two phrases, the norm is to vary the dynamic level. Play the first phrase of section A loudly and the second phrase softly. The same applies to section B. When repeating section A, play the entire section loudly. Remember that dynamics should be restrained.

- As far as phrasing is concerned, play each phrase in one breath. You can experiment with tonguing each note separately or playing each phrase without tonguing.

Menuet en Rondeau

Jean-Philippe Rameau

George Frederick Handel

Handel was one of many composers through the ages whose family insisted that he study law. He had to sneak a clavichord (a soft practising keyboard) into the attic to practise and would be severely reprimanded when caught. Luckily the Duke of Saxe-Weissenfels heard the young Handel playing the organ and persuaded his father to let him follow a musical career. He worked as violinist and harpsichordist in the Hamburg Opera orchestra before going to Italy. This is where his talent for opera composition developed and it is his 40-odd operas that kept him busy and solvent for much of his life.

He moved to London where he was embarrassed when his previous employer, the Elector of Hanover, who had never dismissed him from his service, became his 'new' employer as King George I of England. Luckily Handel assuaged the king's animosity by writing the famous Water Music, which pleased the king so much that he even gave him a raise. Although he was well respected in his adopted country, Handel faced many financial problems when the public taste for Italian Opera disappeared. He shifted his focus to sacred composition rather late in his life, and it is for his sacred oratorios like 'Messiah' that he is best remembered.

George Frederick Handel
1685–1759

PLAYING NOTES

- The HWV number refers to the Handel Werke Verzeichnis (the Catalogue of Handel's Works).
- A Sarabande was originally a lively Spanish dance. When it became used in the aristocratic courts, it slowed down considerably and became a very stately affair. The nobility obviously preferred to keep their vigour off the dance floor and conserve it for the boudoir. It has three beats to the bar and (strangely) the second beat is usually emphasized.
- The composer has already compensated for the slow tempo by using bigger note values. Therefore it can be played Andante.
- The key signature says that all B's should be flattened.
- The only accidentals in this piece are the C-sharps in bars 8 and 14. Remember that they only apply to these specific bars.
- Because there are no dynamic markings, look at the music itself. There are two climax points in the melody – in bar 8 and bar 15. To emphasize these climax points, make a slight crescendo (gradually louder) towards them. See it as the build-up of tension and then relaxation. The rest of the piece can be played softly.
- Articulate (tongue) each note except for the notes at the end of the piece under the slur. Tongue at the beginning of each slur.
- This is a very famous tune by Handel and is very beautiful. It will sound especially good on the clarinet or saxophone.

Sarabande

HWV/IV

George Frederick Handel

THE 18TH CENTURY

It is very important to realize that changes in musical thought (or any thought for that matter) did not happen overnight. Even though we are now focusing on the 18th century, there are many aspects of the previous century which still prevailed in this one. Change took place at different speeds in different locations and any historian knows that it is useless to agonize over specific dates that mark the beginning and end of certain styles or musical developments. In this book, the discussion of the history of Western music is divided into centuries as an arbitrary way of establishing the passage of time, but it should not be seen as creating finite boundaries. Another aspect, which concerns the study of history, is that many concepts have a linear existence that run parallel to one another and combine in different ways to form focus points in the time stream upon which the eyes of the student may rest. One of these focus points, which became especially important in the second half of the 18th century, is the so-called Enlightenment.

As early as the second decade of the century, changes in musical taste became more noticeable. It is particularly during this time that you see a typical characteristic of artistic development. Some hold on to older values while, at the same time, others start embracing progressive trends. Bach serves again as a good example of this. His sons, many of whom became well-known composers themselves, though they had great respect for their father's skill in the 'older' style, often referred to their father's music as 'old-fashioned'. But what did this 'new' style of music entail? Where the previous style was often quite complex, progressive musicians longed for greater simplicity. This started with the so-called Rococo style,

A painting depicts Wolfgang Amadeus Mozart, aged six, sitting with the Empress at the Vienna Imperial Court. Mozart performed here as a child prodigy in the 1760s.

which strove towards grace, wit, elegance and the sole purpose of pleasing the refined sensibilities of the listener. This caused a gradual 'lightening' in the texture of the music.

While the Rococo signalled the beginning of the artistic Enlightenment, the writings of Voltaire, Thomas Paine and Jean-Jacques Rousseau signalled the beginning of the intellectual Enlightenment. This philosophy strove to raise the level of general education so that obsessions with the supernatural could be redirected towards human betterment. This was not an ideal situation for either the aristocratic or clerical institutions, which relied heavily on divine sanction in order to justify their importance. It can be argued that the spread of this movement led to the destruction of the aristocratic institutions during the French Revolution (1789–99), which forever changed the social structure of Europe.

One aspect of the Enlightenment was the rediscovery and renewed interest in classical civilizations. It was especially in the architecture of these civilizations that music found its greatest inspiration. Composers wished to have the same balance and symmetry in their works, and they exchanged the complications of the past for simple, yet effective harmonic, melodic and formal structures in their music. It was in the latter half of the 18th century that melody became the supreme force in musical composition. This is why the clarinet developed and became popular in this time: it presented composers with a whole new range of sound and expression which they could utilize in their compositions. Mozart made

FAMOUS COMPOSERS

1714–1787	Christoph Willibald Gluck
1714–1788	Carl Philip Emaneul Bach
1732–1809	Franz Joseph Haydn
1735–1782	Johann Christian Bach
1743–1805	Luigi Boccherini
1745–1801	Carl Stamitz
1752–1832	Muzio Clementi
1756–1791	Wolfgang Amadeus Mozart
1770–1827	Ludwig van Beethoven
1778–1837	Johann Nepomuk Hummel

the famous remark, after having heard the well-known orchestra of Mannheim, that he wished their orchestra in Salzburg had clarinets too. It was the Mannheim orchestra which served as the model for the 'modern' form of the symphony orchestra, which is arguably the biggest musical development to take place during the 18th century. Since this orchestra had a pair of clarinets, it meant that the clarinet became a regular feature of all later symphony orchestras.

The rise of the symphony orchestra also coincided with, and helped shape, the development of the symphony. This is a large-scale, multi-movement work for symphony orchestra which developed out of the opera overture (the bit that the orchestra plays before the beginning of the opera to set the mood and give the audience a chance to settle down). Another important ensemble (group) in which the clarinet featured prominently was the so-called 'Harmoniemusik'. This was an early kind of military band (see p80), consisting mostly of wind instruments like oboes, bassoons and horns, which could be found at any large musical establishment. It is usually from the ranks of this group that players were found to play the clarinet parts in a symphony orchestra.

The Enlightenment also manifested itself in the growth of the public concert. Most musical activities up until this time were sponsored either by court or church, but because of their decline, the public started taking over the patronage of music. It is in these surroundings that composers like Mozart could perform their works for a paying audience.

PLAYING NOTES

- Composers became more specific in this century when indicating dynamics in their music. The most important aspect in this regard is moderation. When dynamic change does occur, it is usually more gradual and not too drastic.

- Melody is the most important aspect of the music in this time. Since the clarinet and saxophone are melodic instruments, this means that your part must be heard above the accompaniment.

- The most important kind of improvisation in this time is the cadenza, which is an improvised section played by the soloist in a concerto (see p77). The cadenza must usually contain elements of the main composition.

The Rococo style in music echoed the gaiety of the *fête champêtre* – or 'country celebration' – in 18th-century paintings. This work by Johann Heinrich Schmidt, entitled 'Dancing in the Open Air', is dated 1741.

Ludwig van Beethoven (1770–1827)

Beethoven's alcoholic father had no intention of making a lawyer of his son. He recognized his son's musical talent, but tried to make a second Mozart of him, something which was equally traumatic and earned the young boy many a beating. He worked as a musician in the electoral chapel in Bonn, but then moved to Vienna. Here, he made the acquaintance of Mozart and Haydn, the two masters of the so-called classical style. It is also here that he became the first freelance musician – never again working for court, church or deferring to people of higher social rank. His unpredictable temper and bad manners were excused by his wealthy friends and patrons as a sign of his artistic temperament. He established himself as one of the best pianists in Vienna, the musical capital of Europe at the time. Despite his advancing deafness, he continued to write a great deal of large-scale works as well as music of an intensely intimate character.

From the time of Beethoven it became more common for a composer or his publisher to give his own works opus numbers. This is symptomatic of the new identity of the artist – free from aristocratic or clerical patronage.

Ludwig van Beethoven
1770–1827

PLAYING NOTES

- A catalogue number like this one is often used to number works which were not numbered by the composer, or published after his death, or only discovered by musicologists at a much later date.
- This piece has no tempo indication. But the term maggiore refers to the fact that this variation is now again in the major key (the previous variation was in the minor) and should contrast with the previous one. Major and minor are aspects of tonality (see glossary). There is no simple explanation for what major and minor are, but for now it is sufficient to think of major as 'happy' and minor as 'sad'. Since the previous variation was 'sad', slow and legato, this one should be lively, fast and articulated.
- The time signature which looks like a C is another way of writing 4/4 – that is, four quarter notes to a bar.
- Remember to flatten all B's – a nice big hammer should do the trick (just kidding).
- The beginning of the variation is marked forte (loud) and since no other dynamic markings occur, the entire variation should be played forte.
- Once again, all notes are tongued unless they are under a slur. The staccato notes (those with a dot above the note) should be tongued quickly and vigorously. Make sure to observe the breathing indication.

Variation on a Swiss Song

WOO 64

Variation 4
Maggiore

Ludwig van Beethoven

Carl Maria von Weber

Carl Maria von Weber was yet another child whose father was adamant that he should be the next *wunderkind* after Mozart. Luckily, this pressure on the young boy was more constructive than it had been with Beethoven. Carl's father, a bit of an eccentric who had appropriated the title of *Baron von* Weber from an extinct Austrian noble family, quit his work as city musician and began his own travelling theatre company, consisting mostly of his family. Carl Maria had not been a very robust child – he was afflicted by a congenital hip disorder, which gave him a limp. He worked for a while as conductor in Breslau, but after a misunderstanding which led to the accidental poisoning of a rival, he moved quickly on to Stuttgart, where he worked as a musician in the court of the King of Württemberg. The poor man was even imprisoned for 'borrowing' money from his employer and then paying it back with a loan made possible by an innkeeper who expected Weber to use his influence at the court to free his son from military service by acquiring a post for him there. Yet, despite his initial run of bad luck, Weber managed, with works like his opera *Der Freischütz*, to achieve international recognition as a composer.

Carl Maria von Weber
1786–1826

PLAYING NOTES

- The piece is a trio, which stands between the statement and repetition of a waltz. It is called a trio because there are three 'voices' or parts in the music.
- The trio is usually a bit more relaxed than the two outer movements and the tempo should therefore not be too fast.
- Remember not to confuse your key signature with that of the accompaniment.
- In the beginning, the *p* e legato means you should play as softly (piano) and as smoothly (legato) as possible.
- This is the first piece with proper dynamic markings. Composers towards the end of the 18th century became a bit more specific when writing down their music, since the circulation of their works was wider than in the previous eras. The piece starts piano (softly) with a big crescendo from bar 4 to 9 where it becomes forte (loud). The *fz* (sforzando) is another way of writing a very powerful accent. Do not blow too hard or you will not get the note out of the instrument.
- Articulate exactly as written. Tongue all the notes except for those under the slurs. Remember that hard tonguing will be necessary for the accents and sforzandos.

Trio

Carl Maria von Weber

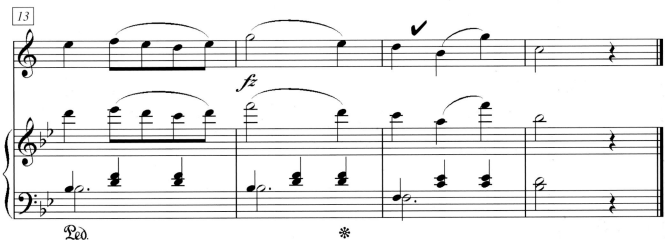

THE 19TH CENTURY

It is obvious that all the elegance and rationality of the 18th century would eventually wear the nerves of those of a stormy temperament – this is one of the most fundamental aspects of humanity. In an age where rationality and logic prevails, there will always be those who react against it by propagating a return to nature, the mythical and the supernatural. These tenets gain a wide following until they supplant those of the previous age, only to give rise to a new set of disgruntled individualists who in turn react against the establishment. This never ending see-saw ride is often referred to as the 'classical' temperament versus the 'romantic' temperament. The former seeks rationality and order while the latter seeks emotion and fantasy.

Signs of the romantic temperament can already be seen in the latter half of the 18th century in the literary movement known as *Sturm und Drang* (Storm and Stress). It delighted in shocking the audience with nightmarish scenes of dungeons and ghosts. One of the first composers to take up the flag of 'romanticism', which was to become the main artistic stream of the 19th century, was Ludwig van Beethoven (1770–1827). He is a perfect example to illustrate the gradual change from 'classicism' to Romanticism. His early works have the same clarity and elegant simplicity of Mozart's, but many of his latter

The Romantics' obsession with mysticism and nature found expression in many paintings which lauded pastoral simplicity.

works become stormy, temperamental and violent. This has a lot to do with the changing circumstances of the composer.

Beethoven, like Mozart, started his musical career as a servant of the church, where he was expected to produce a certain 'kind' of music. With the decay and fall of the aristocracy, the ensuing power vacuum was filled by rich individuals who also took over the patronage of the arts. Mozart was unlucky enough to find himself in this uncertain time, which explains how such a musical genius could not find regular employment and eventually died in poverty at the age of 35. Beethoven, a mere 14 years Mozart's junior, was able to pursue and sustain a freelance career, which afforded him the opportunity to write music that suited his own artistic temperament. In this sense, Beethoven is seen as the first true 'romantic' and he was venerated by later composers as the father of Romantic music.

This veneration, which translated into hero-worship, is still a characteristic of the music industry. Most people forget that these great composers of the past were people too. They had to pay the rent, they had to feed themselves and they also had to make regular visits to the privy. It is important to divest the man of the accumulated clutter of myths and legends that surround him if you wish to understand his music. This is difficult to achieve with composers who lived before the 19th century, of whom few personal documents survive. It is, however, even more difficult to discover the man behind the music when dealing with composers of the 19th century, as

PLAYING NOTES

- Composers start using very colourful terminology to describe the kind of feeling they want their music to convey. This includes unrestrained use of dynamic and interpretive signs.
- While melodies are just as important in the 19th century, they are far more individualistic and recognizable.
- Since composers were quite specific when writing down their music, chances for improvisation are rather limited.

This caricature, by A. Theuerkauf, of composer Franz Liszt conducting, shows the typical Romantic artist – hypersensitive, and not always in touch with the world around him.

building took place in this time, since makers were hoping to capitalize on this craze. It is in this time that the saxophone developed, which explains its immense popularity.

The rise of Romanticism also caused a surge in individuality and originality in composition. In the 17th century, musical styles could be 'defined' in terms of national boundaries such as the 'Italian' or 'French' style. In the 18th century, music could be defined in terms of 'movements', such as the Rococo and Sturm und Drang, or 'schools' such as the 'first Viennese school', which includes the music of Haydn, Mozart, and the early works of Beethoven, all of whom had intimate connections with this city. In the 19th century, however, each composer had his own unique style. This does not mean that there were no similarities between the music of different composers, but that it is easier to distinguish between, for example, Brahms and Wagner than it is to distinguish between Haydn and Mozart.

many of their actions were sensationalized beyond credibility. A few examples include Niccolò Paganini (1782–1840), who was rumoured to have sold his soul to the devil in exchange for his amazing prowess on the violin. Another is Franz Liszt (1811–86), the 'Paganini of the Piano', who apparently paid young ladies to fall into hysterics or to swoon at the sound of his playing. Nevertheless, all these accounts do make for entertaining reading.

What kind of music thrived in these turbulent surroundings? The answer is: every imaginable kind, from intimate works for solo piano to monstrous orchestral works that prompted many cartoonists to include cannons in their depiction of an orchestra.

During the 19th century, it was once again seen as a social accomplishment to be able to play a musical instrument, and it was no longer limited to the aristocratic sphere. This was made possible by the greater availability of cheap instruments and the growth of an affluent middle class after the industrial revolution. This is why most developments in instrument

FAMOUS COMPOSERS

1792–1868	Gioachino Antonio Rossini
1797–1828	Franz Schubert
1803–1869	Hector Berlioz
1809–1847	Felix Mendelssohn
1810–1849	Frédéric Chopin
1810–1856	Robert Schumann
1811–1886	Franz Liszt
1813–1883	Richard Wagner
1813–1901	Giuseppe Verdi
1824–1884	Bedrich Smetana
1825–1899	Johann Strauss II
1833–1897	Johannes Brahms
1835–1921	Camille Saint-Saëns
1838–1875	Georges Bizet
1840–1893	Pyotr Ilyich Tchaikovsky
1841–1904	Antonin Dvořák
1843–1907	Edvard Grieg
1844–1908	Nikolai Andreyevich Rimsky-Korsakof
1857–1934	Edward Elgar
1860–1911	Gustav Mahler
1864–1949	Richard Strauss
1865–1931	Carl Nielsen
1865–1936	Alexander Konstantinovich-Glazunov
1869–1937	Albert Roussel

Robert Schumann

Despite some early signs of musical creativity, Schumann showed much more interest in literature and writing. His fame as a music critic and writer preceded his fame as a composer. This is due to his father's library, which featured many 'dark' fantasies which the young Schumann avidly devoured. After the death of his father, Schumann was coerced into the legal profession (like so many before and after him), but he did not care much for this, indulging rather in all the excesses that student life afforded him. Here he realized that his true calling lay with music and that he wished to become a concert pianist. After dislocating a finger using a device that was supposed to strengthen it, Schumann turned instead to musical criticism and composition.

He married Clara, the daughter of his piano teacher (much to the latter's dismay), who was an excellent pianist herself, and it is for her that many of his works were written. Unfortunately, Schumann's mental health deteriorated, causing him to alternate between hugely creative and dark depressed periods. After trying to drown himself, he spent the last two years of his life in an asylum.

Robert Schumann
1810–56

PLAYING NOTES

- The choral(e) is not the most typical Romantic form. This one forms part of a collection of works that Schumann published for young players in which he emphasizes how important it is for a young person to be exposed to 'good' music. At the end of the work, he gives a list of 'Musical Rules at Home and in Life'. This is a fascinating document and is highly recommended by the author.
- The piece should be played at a moderate pace, neither too slow nor too fast. Although people think that church chorales should be slow and solemn, we must remind ourselves that they were originally passionate songs to the Lord and sung with great vigour by early Protestant congregations.
- The time signature that looks like a C with a vertical line through it is another way of writing 2/2, or two half note beats to a bar.
- Remember to flatten all B's. There are no accidentals.
- The piece starts piano, but the player should increase the volume as the melody rises. Bear in mind that a melody's natural climax lies with the highest notes.
- The phrases are long and legato. Tongue only the beginning of each phrase. The upside-down half circle with a dot in it is called a fermata. This indicates a pause, where the note is held for longer than normal and a sufficient break occurs in order to breathe – remember that the 'congregation' singing in the church also has to breathe.

Choral

Op. 68/IV

Robert Schumann

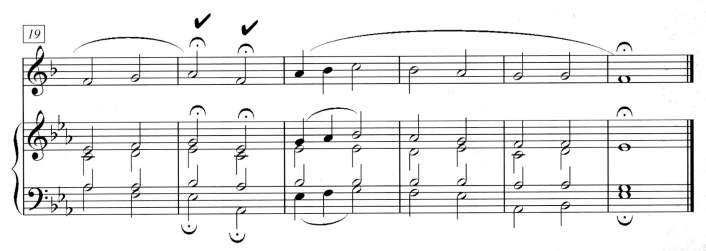

Johannes Brahms

Brahms, who is better known as the last of the 'three great Bs' in musical composition (which includes Bach and Beethoven), was born in Hamburg and was lucky to have a father who was more interested in music than law. He received his initial piano instruction from his father and went on to play dance music in brothels as a teenager. After hearing him play, the famous violinist Joseph Joachim sent him off with letters of introduction to Liszt and Schumann. Liszt was not impressed with Brahms because he fell asleep while the older pianist was showing off, but Schumann proclaimed Brahms 'the saviour of German music'.

This was quite a weight to shoulder and might explain why Brahms only completed his first symphony 20 years after he had started it. During this time, the musical public was strongly divided into progressive and traditionalist camps. Brahms was often caught in the crossfire because he straddled the two. He employed the progressive musical vocabulary of the day, but he never abandoned the formal organization of the preceding era. This is why Hans von Bülow, the famous orchestral conductor, on hearing Brahms's first symphony, proclaimed it to be Beethoven's tenth.

Johannes Brahms
1833–97

PLAYING NOTES

- This is the second of a set of waltzes written by the composer. The first is soulful and melancholic while the second is in a light and playful vein. These waltzes were not written to be danced to, and were originally for the piano. The indication poco scherzando means 'slightly joking'. Leggiero means 'lightly'.
- The piece is in two sections, each of which is repeated. At the end of the first playing, the ending under the first bracket is played. At the end of the repeat, the ending under the second bracket is played.
- Remember to flatten the B's. There are many accidentals in this piece. Make sure that you know which notes you should play. Remember that the bar line enforces the key signature.
- Note the crescendos and decrescendos. When you are playing the melody (the eighth notes), they apply to you. When you play the accompaniment (the staccato quarter note bars 5 to 7), you should play more softly than the melody.
- As far as articulation is concerned, the melodic bits are played legato while the accompaniment sections are played staccato.

Waltz

Op. 39 No. 10

Johannes Brahms

20TH CENTURY (CLASSICAL)

The musical individuality of the 19th century caused a 'problem' to develop in the early stages of the 20th century. Originality was highly praised, but because of the limited musical vocabulary of the time, 'classical' composers found that, no matter how hard they applied themselves, their works were constantly being branded as reactionary because they sounded like something that had been written before. This 'problem' was partially resolved by composers belonging to the so-called 'second Viennese school', namely Arnold Schoenberg (1874–1951), Alban Berg (1885–1935) and Anton Webern (1883–1945). They started rejecting traditional tonality in favour of a system where no key predominated. This 'free' atonality pushed back the boundaries of musical expression and laid the foundations for entirely new developments.

FAMOUS COMPOSERS

1862–1918	Claude Debussy
1872–1958	Vaughan Williams
1873–1943	Serge Rachmaninov
1874–1951	Arnold Schoenberg
1875–1937	Maurice Ravel
1881–1945	Béla Bartók
1882–1971	Igor Stravinsky
1891–1953	Serge Prokofiev
1898–1937	George Gershwin
1906–1974	Dmitri Shostakovich
1912–1992	John Cage
1913–1976	Benjamin Britten
b.1928	Karlheinz Stockhausen
b.1935	Arvo Pärt
b.1937	Philip Glass

COMPOSERS FOR SAX/CLARINET

1883–1945	Anton Webern
1890–1962	Jacques Ibert
1901–1956	Gerald Finzi
b.1908	Elliot Carter
1913–1994	Witold Lutoslawski
1930–1996	Toru Takemitsu
b.1933	Krzysztof Penderecki

Once again, it is important to realize that not all composers embraced these new ideals. Some, like Richard Strauss (1864–1949), were quite happy to continue writing in a fairly traditional musical idiom far into the 20th century. Progressive musicians, on the other hand, started a trend of experimentation which has lasted to the present day. One of the first styles, which forms the stepping stone between traditional tonality and atonality, is Impressionism. The term, which originated in the world of the visual arts, describes a style that is vague and seeks to convey impressions rather than concrete facts. The musical exponent of this style was Claude Debussy (1862–1918), who was influenced by the sounds and textures of the music of the near and far East, as were many other artists in the late 19th and early 20th centuries.

Another important development was the continuing influence of nationalism. After the fall of the European aristocracies in the 19th century, the subsequent restructuring of European societies led to a growth in nationalist feeling. This meant that ordinary people started referring to themselves as English, Italian, French, and German. The Feudal system of the Middle Ages had been replaced by democracies, but these new developments were not without teething problems, and caused immense pain and suffering during the two World Wars. Musically speaking, the picture was not so bleak, and huge efforts were made to collect and preserve the folk heritage of different regions. Composers who were especially active in this regard were the English composer, Ralph Vaughan Williams (1872–1968), and the Hungarian composers Béla Bartók (1881–1945) and Zoltán Kodály (1882–1967).

The 20th century also saw the maturation of a trend that originated in the 19th century. In 1829, Felix Mendelssohn performed the 'St Matthew Passion' by Bach (which left even Nietzsche wondering if there was a God); this helped to rekindle an interest in older music. Until this time, musicians and audiences only concerned themselves with music that had been recently written. The older music was seen as an ancient relic fit for perusal only by academics.

As interest in older music increased, older works started featuring next to their contemporary counterparts on musical programmes. Older traditions also started infiltrating modern compositions and gave rise to styles labelled 'neoclassicism' and 'neoromanticism'. Unfortunately, the experiments of the 20th century alienated many listeners, who became more interested in jazz and associated popular styles (see p68). This has led to the modern situation where classical musicians concentrate 98 per cent of their efforts on the performance of 'old' music. Luckily, many contemporary composers, especially those who write music for films, have found new and inspiring ways to utilize traditional methods to create new, exiting, but above all, listener-friendly music. This has helped to rekindle the dwindling interest in classical music. Yet we should not be disdainful of the experimentation that took place in the 20th century, for it is through the efforts of these musicians and composers that the language of music was fully explored and still continues to evolve.

This has been especially exciting if one looks at the advances made in the different sounds that are possible for clarinet and saxophone. Some of these include biting on the reeds to produce a shrill squeaking sound. Another is the use of multiphonics, where unorthodox fingering leads to the simultaneous sounding of two notes. Another interesting effect is created by singing into the instrument while you play, which not only causes two different melodies to sound, but also causes a strange buzzing sound.

If you have any interest in electronics and computers, you will be amazed at some of the advances that have been made, which include electronically altered sounds and computer programs which 'compose' works in the style of famous composers.

PLAYING NOTES

- Due to a lack of common performance practices, composers become so specific in indicating mood, tone-colour and tempo, one can hardly see the wood for the trees.
- Melodies are often serial, making use of formulas and mathematical equations to determine their contour.
- One manifestation of improvisation is so-called aleatoric music, where shorthand instructions by the composer serve as the basis for the performer, who is expected to vary each performance. Chance plays a large role in this style.

An early 20th-century wind ensemble, the Chamber Music Society for Wind Instruments, rehearses for a performance.

Aram Khachaturian

Aram Khachaturian
1903–78

Khachaturian, who is seen by most as the most important Armenian composer of the 20th century, came rather late to the world of music. He played in a wind band (see p80) as a youth and went on to study biology – not law. He soon changed to music, focusing on composition and the cello. His music contains many rhythmic and melodic elements of Armenian traditional music, which he assimilated as a child from listening to his mother's singing and the folk music of his native country.

He started rising in the official musical structures of the Russian union, but became one of many composers (which include Dmitri Shostakovich and Sergei Prokofiev) to be censured by the government for writing 'formalist' music in 1948. He published a grovelling apology, in which he asks: 'What could be nobler than writing music understandable by our people?' He even wrote an 'Ode in Memory of Stalin' just in case the authorities did not believe him. Despite these difficult circumstances, Khachaturian managed to thrive as a composer. The famous 'Sabre Dance' is from his ballet, *Gayne*. He was also one of the first to write music for film, an interest that he held until the end of his life.

PLAYING NOTES

- The title Andantino, which is also the tempo indication, literally means 'small andante', but has a double meaning of being either faster or slower than andante. This is one of many inconsistencies in the world of music, but in this case it would probably be slightly slower.
- The ritardando in the last bar means that you have to slow down slightly. This has more application to the accompanist than it does to you, so just hold the last note until the accompanist finishes.
- Remember that the time signature is another way of writing 4/4.
- Remember to flatten all B's and note the E-flat accidental in bar 16.
- The dynamic indications are simple, but should be strictly observed.
- Cantabile means to play in a singing manner. This does not mean that you sing while you play, but that your playing should have a singing quality comparable with the human voice.
- This piece is truly a gem of 20th-century composition.

Andantino

Used with the kind permission of Editio Musica Budapest

Aram Khachaturian

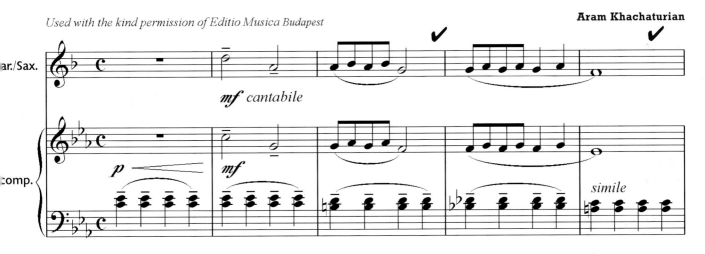

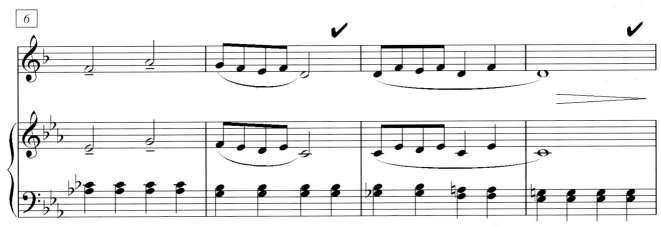

20TH CENTURY (JAZZ)

As you may have noticed, there are many different labels used to describe music. There are two which are notoriously difficult to explain, but need to be clarified before continuing. Up until this point, we have been looking at the history of what is carelessly referred to as 'classical' music. But what do you call all the other types of music like jazz, blues, rock'n'roll and deep funk? These types of music are collectively referred to as 'popular' music, to distinguish it from classical music, which is collectively referred to as 'art' or 'serious' music. You should be able to see that these terms are not very satisfactory, since many popular musicians are very serious about their art, while many serious musicians are immensely popular – but they do help to make sense of the infinite variety that music gives us.

To explore popular music, we have to let our eyes wander away from Europe and settle on North America. It is in the cotton fields of the Southern United States that musical history was being made. African slaves brought with them a vibrant musical culture which relied greatly on singing, dancing, strong rhythms and improvisation. As their traditional rituals became assimilated in the European surroundings of the colonists who had settled there, certain changes started

A street jazz performance in Harlem, New York, reflects the spirit of this form of music – that is, 'music for the people'.

taking place. Drumming soon became outlawed because of the noise and pagan connotations, but it was soon replaced by vigorous clapping and stomping. Plantation owners also introduced the African slaves to European instruments, and soon a new musical culture began to blossom. This started with gospels and spirituals which were sung in the black churches. These were passionate and lively songs, which often had hidden meanings connected with planned escapes from slavery. This gave way to the style known as the 'Blues'. It started out as a way for slaves to express their discontent and was often associated with sex and alcohol, but it became popularized by its dissemination through radio. It was in this era of media development that the blues gained a modicum of respectability. When the young Elvis Presley started 'singing the blues like a black man' in the early 1950s, the blues combined with country music to give us rock'n'roll.

After the American Civil War and the emancipation of the slaves, a more 'optimistic' style, known as 'jazz' developed in and around New Orleans. The term initially had a host of negative associations, but today it is a generic term, much like the term classical, to describe a host of styles and sub-styles which include big band, swing, bebop, free jazz, cool jazz, acid jazz and other musical hybrids. Jazz took over and developed the melodic and harmonic elements of blues and had a radically new approach to rhythm, which includes ample use of syncopation. Improvisation also forms one of the cornerstones of jazz performance. The biggest difference between the blues and jazz, however, was described by Sidney Bechet: 'All that waiting, all that time that song was far-off music

FAMOUS ARTISTS

JAZZ SAXOPHONISTS

Soprano

Sidney Bechet
Branford Marsalis
Andy Sheppard
David Sanborn
Grover Washington Jr.

Stan Getz
Dexter Gordon
Coleman Hawkins
Sonny Rollins
Ben Webster
Lester Young
Courtney Pine

Alto

Ornette Coleman
Johnny Hodges
Charlie Parker
Eric Dolphy
Maceo Parker

Baritone

Harry Carney
Gerry Mulligan

JAZZ CLARINETTISTS

Artie Shaw
Benny Goodman
Pee Wee Russell
Don Byron
Paquito d'Rivera

Tenor

Wayne Shorter
John Coltrane

A 1929 score cover of a piece for saxophone illustrates the world's obsession with this instrument at that time.

[blues], waiting music, suffering music. . . It was joy music now.' Jazz was not seen as such a marketable commodity as the blues, but the popularity of jazz soon increased, and by the 1920s and 1930s it was being recorded and spread through the rest of North America, Latin America and Europe. This new sound was particularly attractive to classical composers like Igor Stravinsky, Dmitry Shostakovich and George Gershwin, who used jazz elements in their compositions.

Initially, jazz had a more functional value in that it provided music for dancing. Later it was to provide entertainment, often with some sort of theatrical element involved. It is in this time that musicians like Louis Armstrong, Duke Ellington, Paul Whiteman and Benny Goodman brought jazz into middle-class households and gave it an air of respectability during the 'big band' and 'swing' eras in the 1930s and 1940s. Now musicians were entertaining listeners and dancers alike, not only in smoky bars, but also in Carnegie Hall. Jazz vocalists also became prominent at this time and included artists like Bing Crosby, Ella Fitzgerald and Frank Sinatra.

After World War II, bands started streamlining and smaller groups began to dominate. Virtuosity also started playing a role, especially since jazz was now finding its way into music schools and conservatories, which caused a profusion in technically brilliant clarinettists and saxophonists. In the 1950s and 1960s a new trend emerged known as 'free jazz' (Ornette Coleman's playing, for example). It was a wild, angry, uncompromising music, played for art's sake (much like the Romantic movement and the later advent of atonality and the classical avant garde). This style was less palatable to the masses, who were focusing on the developments of rock'n'roll.

Parallel with free Jazz, you had 'mainstream jazz'. This 'type' of jazz is still developing as musicians fuse jazz elements with various other styles. This includes the experiments of John McLaughlen with Indian music, and pianist Jacques Lousier, who successfully 'jazzed up' the music of Bach and various other classical composers.

Famous blind sax player Roland Kirk, through superb breath control, was able to play three instruments simultaneously.

George Gershwin

Gershwin, whose parents were Russian immigrants, was born in New York. As a boy, he showed far more interest in athletics and 'spending time with the boys, making somewhat of a nuisance of myself in the streets' than in music. After 'discovering' Rubenstein's 'Melody in F' in a penny arcade on Coney Island, and the subsequent purchase of the family's first piano, Gershwin began a lifelong love-affair with his new interest. At 15 he dropped out of school to work as a 'song plugger' (see glossary) in Tin Pan Alley, where he began writing his own popular songs.

Initial praise for his compositional talents fired his ambition and he left Tin Pan Alley to work as a rehearsal pianist on Broadway. Here he made connections which allowed some of his works to feature on the programmes and after the phenomenal success of his song 'Swanee' (yielding $10,000 in royalties in the first year), he shot to fame. He also developed a passionate interest in classical composition, as his works 'Rhapsody in Blue' and 'An American in Paris' testify.

Gershwin experienced wealth and fame in abundance, but the world was shocked when in 1937 he fell suddenly into a coma, caused by a brain tumour. He died a few days later at the age of 38.

George Gershwin
1898–1937

PLAYING NOTES

- When playing a transcription of a popular song, it is important to place it in context. This song is a lament by a mother to her young child. Despite the fact that she is a slave on a cotton plantation, she sings to the child of the perfect world in which she imagines them to be. It is very tragic, but this version is slightly more upbeat.
- The emotional content corresponds with the tempo indication — at a slow speed and with expression. The sign next to it is a very specific way of indicating how many quarter notes per minute should be played. This is a very frequent indication in modern composition (see p26).
- Poco animato (bar 8) means 'slightly animated', which in turn means that the tempo should be increased slightly.
- Remember to flatten all B's and E's.
- This piece, like most pieces in the jazz style, is very complicated rhythmically. Take some extra time to make sure that you understand the rhythm of the piece. ⌐3⌐ in bars 6, 10, 14 and 17 is called a triplet (also referred to as 'swing time'). This means that the three notes under the bracket should be played in the same time it would take to play two notes of the same value. In practical terms, it is a 'lazy' way of playing ♩♩.
- Put some soul into this piece.

Summertime

from *Porgy and Bess*

George Gershwin

When the Saints go Marching in (Spiritual)

Spirituals are religious songs, sung in a style that originated in the Deep South of the United States of America. They form one of the greatest folk heritages of American music and have maintained their popularity to this day. Initially, these songs were sung at black church gatherings or sometimes at slave meetings, where many of the texts, such as 'Steal Away', would have veiled references to their escape from bondage. These songs were often slow and melancholy and called 'sorrow songs', which establish their affinity to the blues tradition. Many of them, however, could be very lively and are often called 'jubilees'. Some aspects of the style include singing in unison, alternation between a leader and chorus, stamping, hand-clapping and shouting. The style became well known to the international community after the various concert tours of the Jubilee Singers from Nashville, Tennessee, which started in 1871. Since the Deep South was also the birthplace of jazz, we can understand that the styles would influence one another. This is why 'When the Saints go Marching in' is just as much a jazz anthem as it is a spiritual.

The late 19th century saw a crossover of influences between spirituals and jazz.

PLAYING NOTES

- Try to communicate the same joyful exuberance of this piece that's complemented by the jazz character of the arrangement.
- Most spirituals do not have a known composer, but you now have some information on the history and style to help form your interpretation.
- The tempo indication is quite specific regarding the character of the piece.
- Again, flatten all B's. There are no accidentals (unless you decide to add a few to spice up improvisation).
- The rhythm of your part has been kept as simple as possible, but that does not stop you from experimenting with syncopation as has been done in bar 16.
- There are many ties (see p27) in this piece. It is not necessary to hold each note for its whole value otherwise you will have no chance to breathe. Make sure to follow the breathing indications. If you are not happy with these, you are at liberty to decide on your own breathing. Just make sure that you do it in musical places.
- Where the accompaniment is higher (bars 11 to 14), you can play slightly softer.

When the Saints go Marching in

Spiritual
Arranged: Philip du Toit

chapter five

DEVELOPING YOUR LISTENING SKILLS

OF ALL OUR SENSES, HEARING IS THE MOST NEGLECTED by today's society. We speak to each other without really listening; we tune out modern noise which would have had those living in the Victorian Age running for earplugs; we generally go through life without taking the time to listen to someone breathing — or simply to delight in silence.

Playing a musical instrument or taking an active part in making music helps us to regain and develop our precious sense of hearing, because it forces us to listen. This listening can take place on two levels. Passive listening, on the one hand, is something you do everyday, (often without realizing it), and includes listening to elevator music, the background music to movies and taking absent-minded notice of the radio. Although it is background noise, you would notice if it stopped. In this instance, the music is of secondary importance. In actual fact, music has a powerful emotional influence. Many studies during the past 50 years have shown that certain types of music can help you concentrate better while you're working or studying; it can even complement the body's healing processes.

When listening to music is your main focus, on the other hand, it is referred to as active listening. This kind of listening requires active participation and is usually more analytical in nature: you listen to the melody, the lyrics, and assess the difference between the verses and the refrain of the song. These aspects or 'parameters' of music (which also include rhythm, tempo, dynamics, tone colour, harmony and form) are tools that help the brain to make sense of what the ears are hearing. Although you often enjoy music more because you've heard the piece before, and the familiarity makes you comfortable with it, it is much better to vary your listening and experience as much unknown music as possible. A lot of active listening will also complement the process of interpretation (see previous chapter).

With a limited vocabulary, it is difficult to express yourself adequately in any language — and it's the same with music. This chapter gives information on the various parameters of music to give you the necessary tools you need to understand and appreciate music on another level. It also acquaints you with musical traditions that are centuries old, and encourages you, as a budding clarinettist or saxophonist, to take part in them.

OPPOSITE The term 'military', given to marching bands playing woodwind, brass and percussion, was incorrectly applied to 'civilian' bands. Today the term 'mixed wind band' is used.

INSTRUMENTAL MUSIC

Since ancient times, instrumental music has been divided into two distinct categories, whose roots lie in the musical practices of Ancient Greece. There, they made a clear distinction between stringed instruments such as the lyre (associated with the intellectual and philosophical cult of Apollo, god of music) and wind instruments like the *aulos*, an ancestor of the oboe (associated with the ecstatic and frenzied rites of the cult of Dionysus, Greek god of wine and inspiration). In medieval times, this distinction between instruments was referred to as 'low' and 'high' music. Low (or soft) music described the strings, played for the gentry – usually indoors; high (or loud) music described wind instruments, had more popular appeal and was generally played outside.

During the Renaissance (c.1400–1600), winds were often referred to as 'ignoble' instruments (because of phallic connotations) and the strings as 'noble'. It is no coincidence that Elizabeth I (1533–1603), the Virgin Queen, preferred the soft sound of the strings above all other music. This tradition of separation, which spanned thousands of years, crystallized into two musical ensembles (groups): namely, the orchestra and the band. The orchestra consists mainly of strings and plays music that is softer in general (although it can become quite loud if the conductor cannot control the brass players!). Its music is usually performed in a concert hall and has greater intellectual appeal. The band comes in many shapes and sizes but is usually much louder than the orchestra, plays out of doors and its music has a greater popular appeal.

The two distinct groups are not always comfortable in one another's presence. Famous orchestral conductor, Sir Thomas Beecham, was wont to remark: 'Wind bands are all very well in their place – out of doors and several kilometres away'. To many band players, the orchestral scene appears to be filled with people who are 'arrogant', 'snobbish' and way too serious for their own good!

Luckily, both musical groups have an abundant, rich tradition – and since the clarinet and saxophone are to be found in both groups, you can decide which part of your personality to appeal to: the Apollonic or the Bacchic.

The Concert by A. D. Gabbiani, depicting musicians at the Modena Court, c.1690; strings were always associated with the aristocracy.

THE ORCHESTRA

In a symphony orchestra, clarinettists sit together with the other wind players, situated behind the strings.

In Ancient Greece, the term 'orchestra' referred to ground level in an amphitheatre. In the 17th century, the word was used to describe the area in front of a stage, and since this was where the musicians usually sat, the word was eventually used to describe the players themselves. One of the innovators of the 'modern' orchestra was the composer, Jean-Baptiste Lully (1632–87), who worked at the court of Louis XIV (1638–1715). It was the most fashionable and emulated court in Europe, and Lully's orchestra was widely copied, becoming the standard for a group of musicians.

By the 1740s the orchestra resembled our modern 'symphony' orchestra, whose ensemble is based on the violin family. It includes violins, violas and cellos, divided into groups that play in unison (that is, all playing the same notes). The violins are divided into two groups called first and second violins (no surprise there). Each orchestra usually has a standard number of woodwinds (two flutes, two oboes, two clarinets in B-flat and two bassoons) and brass (two horns). Auxiliary instruments such as piccolos, cor anglais (an alto oboe), clarinets in A- and E-flat, double bassoons, trumpets, trombones, tubas, saxophones and percussion are usually added to suit the instrumental forces required by the composer.

The orchestra is seated in a semi-circle around the conductor, the strings in the front, the woodwinds in the middle and the brass at the back. This ensemble functions mostly in the 'classical' music sphere.

Music for the clarinet and saxophone can be divided roughly into four broad categories: orchestral, chamber, music for solo with accompaniment, and music for solo without accompaniment.

Orchestral music

The wind player has two possible functions when playing with an orchestra: he could be playing one of the parts in a work for orchestra or as a soloist with the orchestra. In the first instance, the works for clarinet far outnumber those for saxophone, but a very famous example of a 'classical' orchestral work that does feature saxophone is the *Bolero* by Maurice Ravel (1875–1937). These works include overtures, symphonies, orchestral dances and tone poems (a type of programme music – see p79).

When the piece features a soloist, the work is called a concerto. This is a piece for the soloist with orchestral accompaniment; the name will usually specify the instrument that takes the solo, the key in which the concerto starts and an opus, or 'work', number – for example, Mozart's *Clarinet Concerto in A major KV 622*. The concerto has always been the domain of the virtuosi (a term referring to technically

A group of chamber music players is composed of a number of soloists, each of whom has his own unique contribution to make.

brilliant players) and many composers have obliged them by writing concertos that can only be played by a musician with superhuman ability. Orchestral music is usually performed in a concert hall, but many orchestras give summer performances in the open air.

Chamber music

The second type of music for the clarinet and saxophone is called chamber music, which refers to a number of soloists playing together. The number and kind of instruments can vary, but they will remain a chamber group or ensemble for as long as they do not need a conductor to keep them together. Twelve players are usually the limit. Once again the clarinet features more prominently in 'classical' chamber music and is found in many different chamber combinations. The most common ones are the clarinet trio (with violin and cello or sometimes piano and cello), the clarinet quartet (with violin, viola and cello) and the clarinet quintet (with string quartet). Chamber music concerts can take place almost anywhere, but usually suit more intimate surroundings than the concert hall offers. If you have a few friends who can play the relevant instruments, such a concert could even be held in your own living room.

Solo with accompaniment

There is a huge amount of music for the soloist. Many such pieces were originally written for clarinet or saxophone, but there is also an abundance of transcriptions of pieces that were not intended for these instruments. So even if your favourite tune was composed for trumpet, for example, the chances are good that you will find a clarinet or saxophone transcription of the same piece (see p91).

As difficult as it is to pigeonhole something as diverse and complex as music, pieces for soloist and accompaniment can be divided into the following categories: a piece in a specific musical form, a piece conveying a certain mood, or a piece that was written to develop a specific technical ability. The first includes works like rondos (where the main theme A alternates with secondary, contrasting themes B and C, often following the pattern ABACA); theme and variations (where a recognizable theme is played and then varied in a number of ways); fugues (a type of multi-voiced writing where a theme is stated in one voice and then repeated and imitated by a succession of other voices); and sonatas.

The sonata is probably the most important genre in this category and requires an explanation. It got its name from the Italian *suonare*, which refers to a piece that is 'played' as opposed to a piece that is sung (*cantata*). It is a multi-movement work, usually consisting of three movements: fast-slow-fast. The first movement is usually in sonata-form where a main theme and secondary theme are stated in the first part (exposition), altered and developed in the second part (development), after which the recapitulation restates the exposition with minor alterations.

The second category for soloist accompaniment, where works bear descriptive titles, is often referred to as programme music. The works are usually inspired by extra-musical things like nature, lovers or wine and serve to convey the composer's emotional (if somewhat intoxicated) reaction to these inspirational sources. Programme music has been around for a long time, but it became especially important during the 19th century. It includes generic titles such as polonaises (Polish dances) and nocturnes (night scenes), but the titles can also be quite specific like *Kinderszenen* (children scenes). Although extra-musical influences were usually an inspiration during composition, a work is only considered to be programme music if the composer himself gave it the descriptive title. Works like Beethoven's 'Moonlight' sonata and Haydn's 'Surprise' symphony are not considered programme music, since these 'nicknames' were given to them by enthusiastic individuals who wanted to describe their own emotional experience when hearing the pieces or as a means of differentiating similar works by the same composer.

The last category concerns works that were written to enhance a specific technical aspect of playing the clarinet or saxophone (or any woodwind instrument, for that matter). These include toccatas (touch pieces) and études (studies).

When performing with an accompanist, the soloist should strive to remain in contact with that performer since, together, they function as a musical unity.

Bear in mind that, simply because a piece has a teaching function, this does not necessarily mean that it is of mediocre quality – although many should be banned or burned for being excessively boring!

Solo without accompaniment

There are not many pieces written specifically for solo clarinet or saxophone (most being transcriptions of flute and cello pieces), and many will conform to the types that have been discussed above.

The pieces that do exist are usually very difficult, the reason being that both the clarinet and saxophone are melodic instruments that can only play one note at a time. This means that the composer (who has to know the instrument very well) would have written a 'multi-layered' melody that includes the bass line and implied harmonies. Needless to say, it is quite difficult to concentrate on all the layers and make sense of it for the listener.

Clarinets and saxophones play an indispensable part in most marching bands.

THE BAND

The band started as a military institution. In ancient times, louder wind instruments were used on the battlefields to pass commands to the soldiers and to inspire them in battle. This military aspect continued throughout the ages.

The 'modern' band originated in medieval times, when it consisted of watchmen who used their instruments for a variety of purposes such as signalling or welcoming dignitaries to the town with a loud fanfare. They were also called upon to provide music for dancing, banquets and religious or secular processions.

The clarinet was first introduced into the band in the mid-18th century and formed an integral part of the *Harmoniemusik* (see p53) from that time onward. The saxophone was created as a band instrument in approximately 1845. As wind instruments developed, they became easier to play – especially brass. During the Industrial Revolution, factory-produced instruments were abundant, relatively cheap and therefore became immensely popular among the working classes. This was also the time of colonial expansion, so these European music traditions were exported worldwide. Band traditions flourished in countries like India (which has an estimated 500,000–800,000 people playing in bands) and the USA (which, according to a 1973 survey had 50,000 secondary-school bands and 2000 ensembles at institutions of higher learning).

Bands can be roughly divided into four categories, each with their own repertoire, instrumentation and function: these are military, 'civilian' or mixed wind, jazz, and 'popular' or rock bands.

Military bands

Even though most bands through the ages can be classified as 'military', the term only started applying to an ensemble from the late 18th century onwards, and referred to a group of regimental musicians playing woodwind, brass and percussion instruments. Since most 'civilian' bands have the same make-up, the term 'military band' was erroneously used to describe those bands too. Only later did the term 'mixed wind band' come to refer to civilian bands as distinctive from military bands. Military bands are usually attached to a regiment or division of the army, air force or navy.

They play a wide variety of music suitable for marching, and are an integral part of any military parade or ceremony. They often perform during state occasions, welcoming foreign dignitaries (not much has changed since the Middle Ages!) and tend to serve a propagandist function, playing national anthems and patriotic songs. Military bands are often expected to march while they play; they achieve this by reading from miniature musical scores fastened to a music stand which is attached to the instrument.

Civilian (mixed wind) bands

Civilian bands are the most varied and the most widespread of all the band types. They include bands associated with towns or cities, and often focus around the police or the fire brigade. Cultural societies tend to support a band, as do some industries, many schools and almost all schools of higher learning. In the USA, the popularity of the civilian band was such that, during George Washington's post-war tour through the country, he was met with a band in almost every town and city he visited. These bands are to be found in many places such as amusement parks, sporting events, parades, concerts, civic ceremonies and graduations. Players range in capability from beginners 'young enough to pick up an instrument' to professionals to the aged. The works they play are equally diverse, including popular songs, medleys of perennial favourites, transcriptions of 'classical' pieces for symphony orchestra and many marches, waltzes and patriotic songs. Such is their popularity that bands such as these introduce many people to the works of Mozart, Beethoven and Wagner.

Musician Clarence Clemons (left) lent great charisma to Bruce Springsteen's E Street Band with his energetic performances on the saxophone.

Jazz bands

The jazz band has many different formats, depending on the style of jazz that it is playing. Despite the fact that some of these styles are quite old (some close to a century), they are still played by enthusiastic amateurs and professionals alike. The jazz band originated at the beginning of the 20th century with the Dixie bands of New Orleans. Made up mostly of African Americans, these bands consisted mostly of wind instruments (although piano and double bass were often added) and they fulfilled an outdoor function. As yet there was no standard jazz ensemble, so the size and instrumentation of the band depended upon the musicians available.

Between the 1920s and 1950s, the band was enlarged and developed into the so-called 'big band', with an associated new style that consisted mostly of dance music. It is in this style that jazz greats like Duke Ellington started the tradition of instrumental doubling on woodwind – meaning that, to this day, jazz clarinettists and saxophonists are capable of playing each other's instruments (in all sizes!) as well as their own.

In the 1930s, which saw the rise of 'swing', bands became smaller and more specialized. In the 1940s the saxophone replaced the clarinet as ensemble instrument (something taken over from the military band where clarinets outnumber all the other instruments and feature as the 'violins' of the band), leaving it free to take the solos. The rise of 'bop' ensured the standardizing of the smaller jazz group, while 'cool' and 'West Coast' jazz experimented with various combinations of instruments. 'Free jazz', which developed in the 1960s, 1970s and 1980s, took this experimentation further, using very unusual combinations that included slide whistles and kazoos. These bands can be heard in schools, concert halls, restaurants and jazz clubs.

Popular bands

Rock bands come in various shapes and sizes, but they usually conform to a pattern that consists of four elements: rhythm, bass, harmony and melody. The rhythm is usually supplied by a drum kit while the bass guitar provides the bass line. Rhythm guitars, piano or keyboard generally provide the harmonies of the song, played in a strong, rhythmic fashion. If a clarinet or saxophone features in a rock band, it is usually as a melodic instrument, doubling the melody sung by the voice and providing a solo at various intervals (listen to Tom Jones, Macy Gray, Beck, or Robbie Williams). Otherwise, the lead guitarist will usually play the melodies.

The music played by a popular band is almost always vocal and aimed at the mass market. Even though the clarinet and the saxophone are not used too often (especially since the 1990s), they are especially effective when used as supplementary instruments to spice up the predictable sound of most modern rock bands. Some noteworthy examples are Madness, Sting, Simply Red, Dire Straits and Björk.

LISTENING LIST

Listening to great performances is one of the best ways to develop an interest in music. Here is a list of recommended recordings featuring the clarinet and saxophone:

CLASSICAL CLARINET

Emma Johnson Finzi/Stanford *Clarinet Concertos* (ASV)
Alain Damiens *American Clarinet* (Virgin Classics)
Jon Manasse Weber *Complete Clarinet Music* (Xlnt)
Paul Meyer *French Clarinet Art* (Denon)
Sabine Meyer Weber *Clarinet Concertos* (EMI), Mozart *Clarinet Concerto*/Debussy *Première Rhapsodie*/Takemitsu *Fantasma/Cantos* (EMI)
Ludmila Peterkova Bartok/Khachaturian/Milhaud/Stravinsky *Clarinet Trios* (Supraphon)
Gervase de Peyer Mozart/Brahms *Clarinet Quintets* (Angel), *French Music for Clarinet and Piano* (Chandos)
Richard Stoltzman Brahms/Beethoven/Mozart *Trios for Piano, Clarinet and Cello* (Sony), *The Essential Clarinet* (RCA), Copland *Clarinet Concerto* (RCA)

JAZZ CLARINET

Don Byron *You Are #6* (Blue Note)
Eddie Daniels *Swing Low Sweet Chariot* (Shanachie)
Buddy De Franco *Mr Clarinet* (Universal)
Benny Goodman *The Very Best of* (RCA), *Collectors Edition* (Copland, Bernstein, Stravinsky, Gould, Bartok) (Sony)
Woody Herman *Blowin' Up a Storm: The Columbia Years* (Sony), *Concord Jazz Heritage Series* (Concord Jazz)
Pee Wee Russell *His Best Recordings 1927–44* (Best of Jazz), *Swingin' With Pee Wee* (Milestone)
Artie Shaw *King of the Clarinet 1938-39* (Hindsight)
Various Artists *Clarinet Marmalade: 25 Great Jazz Clarinettists* (ASV)

CLASSICAL SAXOPHONE

Greg Banaszak Glazunov/Villa-Lobos/Dubois/Ibert *Saxophone Concertos* (Centaur)
Philip Glass *Saxophone* (Orange Mountain)
John-Edward Kelly Ibert/Martin/Larsson *Saxophone Concertos* (Arte Nova)
Branford Marsalis *Romances for Saxophone* (Sony)
Pekka Savijoki *The French Saxophone* (Bis)
World Saxophone Quartet *American Jazz Concertos* (Gershwin, Copland, Lake) (Summit Records)

JAZZ SAXOPHONE

Sidney Bechet *The Sidney Bechet Story* (Proper Box)
Michael Brecker *Two Blocks from the Edge* (Impulse)
Ornette Coleman *The Shape of Jazz to Come* (Rhino), *Ornette on Tenor* (Atlantic), *Free Jazz* (Atlantic)
John Coltrane *Giant Steps* (Atlantic), *My Favorite Things* (Atlantic), *Ballads* (Impulse), *A Love Supreme* (Impulse)
Paul Desmond *Take Ten* (RCA), *Take Five* (with the Dave Brubeck Quartet) (CBS)
Eric Dolphy *Out to Lunch* (Blue Note), *The Original Ellington Suite* (Pacific Jazz)
Stan Getz *Jazz Samba* (Verve), *Getz/Gilberto* (Verve), *Sweet Rain* (Verve), *Focus* (Verve)
Dexter Gordon *A Swingin' Affair* (Blue Note)
Coleman Hawkins *Body and Soul* (RCA), *Coleman Hawkins Encounters Ben Webster* (EMI Gold)
Johnny Hodges *Back to Back: Duke Ellington and Johnny Hodges* (Verve), *Passion Flower* (RCA)
Rahsaan Roland Kirk *Verve Jazz Masters* (Verve)
Branford Marsalis *Contemporary Jazz* (Sony Jazz), *The Dark Keys* (Sony Jazz), *Footsteps of Our Fathers* (Rounder)
Gerry Mulligan *Best of the Gerry Mulligan Quartet with Chet Baker* (Blue Note)
Charlie 'Bird' Parker *The Essential Charlie Parker* (Polygram), *Jazz at Massey Hall* (Debut)
Courtney Pine *To the Eyes of Creation* (Universal/Polygram), *Modern Day Jazz Stories* (Mercury)
Sonny Rollins *Saxophone Colossus* (Blue Note)
Andy Sheppard *In Co-Motion* (Polygram)
Wayne Shorter *Juju* (Blue Note), *Speak No Evil* (Blue Note)
Grover Washington, Jr *Ultimate Collection* (Universal)
Ben Webster *King of the Tenors* (Polygram), *Ben Webster Meets Oscar Peterson* (Verve), *Big Ben* (Proper Box)
World Saxophone Quartet *Play Duke Ellington* (Nonesuch)
Lester 'Pres' Young *The Lester Young Story* (Proper Box), *Complete Savoy Recordings* (Savoy Jazz)

OTHER GENRES

Blood Sweat and Tears *Greatest Hits* (Sony)
Fela Kuti *King of Afrobeat* (Talkin Loud)
Manu Dibango *Wakafrika* (Bluemusic)
Bruce Springsteen and the E Street Band *The Wild, The Innocent and the E Street Shuffle* (CBS)

GOING TO THE CONCERT

The live concert is the best place to experience true high-fidelity sound. Even with the best recording equipment, something is always lost in the recording.

Another advantage of a live performance is that there is entertainment for the eye as well as the ear. Since the advent of television and personal computers, we have become very visually oriented, and having something to watch will help you concentrate on the music.

Etiquette

At rock concerts, nobody bats an eyelid if you fling your underwear onto the stage. However, the authorities might feel a little differently if you try this at a classical concert, therefore it's important to know what to do and what not to do so you can focus on the music alone – and not have to worry about when to clap, for instance.

- Be punctual. It is especially unnerving for a soloist when, out of the corner of his eye, he can see someone noisily making his way to his seat. Most concert halls will probably not allow you in if the music has already started. If you are late, listen with your ear to the door. When people clap, that will give you the necessary time to make a dash for your seat.

- When you go to a concert featuring a concerto, try to get seats just to the left of the middle, and four or five rows from the front. Not only will you be able to hear the soloist better, but you will also be able to see the miracles being performed on the instrument.

- Don't expect any sympathy from onlookers if the conductor stops the show and glares at you as you try to silence your ringing mobile phone, your beeping wristwatch or your jangling jewellery. One modern composer *has* written a work for mobile phones and orchestra, but it will probably not feature on that specific evening!

- Do not talk during the concert. Classical music has constantly changing dynamics and you could be caught with your foot in your mouth, in mid-sentence. You will also receive the evil eye from those around you, since they paid their money to listen to the music, not your witty conversation.

- If you are prone to hay fever or have a cold, keep a handy supply of tissues and cough drops ready. Make sure you unwrap the sweets beforehand. The painfully slow unwrapping of a sweet by a well-meaning concertgoer is enough to instil violent thoughts in those around him. If you have to cough, sneeze or blow your nose, try to keep it for the noisy bits or between movements.

- Don't sleep! The soloist and other musicians have spent countless hours rehearsing the music to perfection, and to see their efforts rewarded by your snoring is a great insult.

- When in doubt, listen. This is the golden rule for clapping. There will always be people who know when to clap. In a multi-movement work like a concerto or sonata, you should not clap between movements. However, in a longer work like a ballet or opera, a very good performance by an individual may elicit spontaneous applause from the audience. If you wish to vocalize your appreciation, 'bravo' is appropriate for males and 'brava' for females. (The plural is 'bravi'.)

- At a jazz concert it is permissible to eat, smoke and make conversation during the performance if you are in a restaurant (and in the smoking zone); however, you should not strive to make your conversation heard above the musical entertainment.

- It is also fine to clap during a jazz piece if the soloist has just given a brilliant solo. Similarly, clapping at the end of pieces is good manners, even if you have to stop eating to applaud.

Last Night of the Proms at the Royal Albert Hall, London, is a festive, rousing, and usually informal affair.

chapter six

TAKING YOUR INTEREST FURTHER

THE HUMAN MIND IS A FASCINATING THING. You can go through your whole life without being aware that something exists, only to find yourself confronted with it on every street corner once you have become aware of its existence. When you take up an instrument as a hobby or become interested in playing one, the world changes. These changes do not include earthquakes or flash floods, but refer to the fact that you look at the world with a new consciousness. Suddenly you will start noticing clarinets or saxophones on the radio, television and even in the background music played in shopping centres and in elevators. You might even give more money to the busker on the street! This excitement and initial enthusiasm is very precious and you should endeavour never to lose it.

This is why people take up hobbies and pursue non-work related activities. Not only does it add spice to your life, but it also broadens your frame of reference. This is especially true for adults, who tend not to develop their brain further after the age of 30. The mind must be constantly stimulated – there is a lot of truth in the saying that 'you are never too old to learn'. Soon you will find that you can apply new knowledge in various ways and in various situations – something you couldn't possibly have foretold when you started.

That is the main function of books such as this one. It simply hands the reader the key that will open the door to a whole new series of life experiences. What the reader makes of this key is entirely up to him or her. Hopefully, you have learnt a great deal from this book and you will take this newfound knowledge and apply it in such a way that it will enrich your life.

If you wish to take this interest further, you will have to consider buying or hiring an instrument, then finding and paying a teacher to give you lessons and teach you to play it properly. But both of these steps can present financial and intellectual pitfalls, especially if they are not well considered beforehand and pursued with care. This chapter hopes to give you the necessary information that will help you in these decisions, giving you various tips and advice to make your search an enjoyable and hassle-free experience. It will also give you some advice on how to expand your music-making experience by playing with other people in a band, orchestra, or any other musical group.

OPPOSITE: A new instrument in a glass case is beautiful – and utterly tempting – but it is better to shop around before committing yourself to a purchase.

GETTING STARTED

The financial minefield that buying an instrument presents has put off many keen beginners. They also often approach a teacher with great enthusiasm only to leave soon after, in a cloud of disillusionment because they feel the teacher does not understand their needs. Don't doubt it, myself and many others before me have experienced the same problems, and have learnt a thing or two in the process.

The most important thing to do is decide, at the outset, what you wish to achieve. Reading books on the subject and asking knowledgeable people about music and the clarinet or saxophone is a step in the right direction. Having some kind of goal in mind will ensure you don't waste too much time and money. A good starting point is to establish what music you would like to play. Remember, however, that you will have to go through a learning curve of trying out all styles of music before you can truly settle on your favourite kind of music and specialize. Therefore, it's important to be patient, especially in the beginning. You have to first learn to play the notes before you can launch into playing your favoured music.

Apart from having patience, you also have to be shrewd when selecting an instrument and teacher. A bad instrument is not going to get you to play well and a bad teacher won't

If you're not sure about how serious your interest is going to be, it's advisable to hire a clarinet or saxophone first.

inspire you in any way. And always focus on your goal. It is the one thing that will propel you through any difficulties you may encounter. You also want to enjoy your new pursuit or there is no point in continuing. Music is also a barometer of your personality — you will learn a great deal about yourself if you pursue it either as a hobby or as a semi-professional.

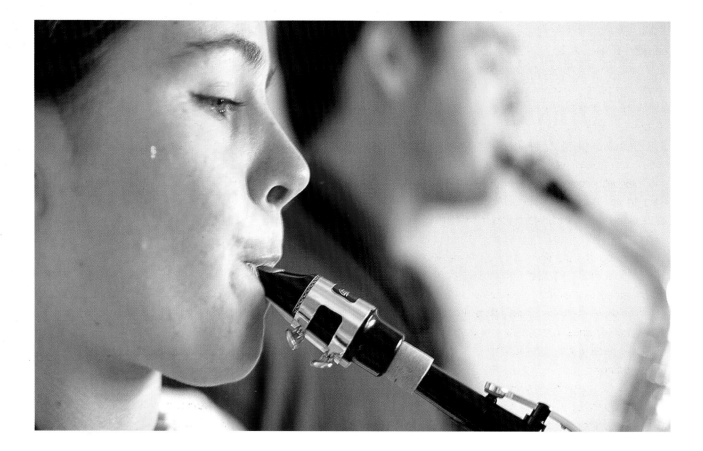

HIRING OR BUYING

If you're not sure whether you're going to maintain your initial enthusiasm, or if money is a problem, the cheapest way to get hold of a clarinet or saxophone is to hire one. Most stores will have instruments that they hire out on a fixed time schedule – usually for three months, six months or even a year. This gives them some control over their stock, enabling them to plan when an instrument can be made available to interested customers. Don't expect a very good instrument, though, since a store will not hire out its best ones. Also expect to pay a deposit, which you will get back when you return the instrument in good working order.

Financially, hiring is an easier option; the disadvantage is, you don't have much control over the quality of the instrument you play. Ask, too, whether insurance and servicing of the instrument have to be handled by yourself or whether the music store covers this. The last thing you want is to be forced to pay for an instrument that has been stolen while in your care. Some stores will give you the choice of hiring a new instrument with the option to buy it later by paying off the outstanding amount.

Buying a second-hand instrument

If you are sure you wish to play a specific instrument, it's advisable to buy your own. Second-hand instruments, whose appearance often is quite alarming, should not be sneered at, because the instrument should be judged by its sound, not its looks. If properly looked after, the advantage is that a second-hand instrument will be easier to handle and will play much better than a brand-new one.

There are many places to look for a second-hand clarinet or saxophone. The first would be music stores. They usually keep second-hand instruments in a back room or storeroom and they will also generally have the details of people who want to sell their instruments. Antique stores are another place to look – but the instruments to be found there will live up to their title!

Another source of information is the classified section of a newspaper or relevant magazine, which usually has advertisements devoted to second-hand instruments. If you cannot find any, putting your own advertisement in the paper is a good idea since many people have an instrument to sell but never really consider it until they come across an interested buyer.

However, it is a perilous quest finding a good second-hand instrument because you don't have the security of guarantees and free maintenance agreements. Therefore it is imperative that you bear the following in mind when buying a second-hand instrument:

- Check for cracks in the wood, plastic or metal of the body of the instrument. If you find any, start looking for another one as they can be quite expensive to repair.
- Take an experienced player with you. He or she will be able to give an opinion on the instrument and judge whether you're being asked to pay more than the instrument is worth.
- Smell the instrument! If it smells terrible, it has probably been poorly looked after.
- Make sure that none of the keys sticks; this means that some springs and other parts may need to be replaced. These replacements will not cost too much if they only need to be made to a few keys, but if the instrument needs an entire overhaul, it could become quite an expensive hobby before you even start playing.
- Listen for the clicking sound of metal against metal when examining the key mechanism. This indicates that keypads are worn and will have to be replaced.

ABOVE Listen for the clicking of metal on metal, which will indicate worn or missing springs & pads.

ABOVE RIGHT Smell the instrument: one that is foul-smelling will have been poorly maintained.

- Make sure that the purchase includes all the necessary accessories like the case, cleaning equipment, mouthpiece guard, ligature, and any paperwork such as guarantees or service records.
- If you are not sure about the price or if you are uncertain about the soundness of the instrument, ask whether it would be possible for you to take it to an expert to have it valued and to ascertain the restoration costs.
- If the instrument is very old, find out whether replacement parts for it are still available. To do this, find out the make and model of the instrument and then phone an instrument supplier with the details.
- Finding out who the previous owner of the instrument was will also give some clue as to its condition. Instruments owned by music students or professional musicians will tend to be in better shape than those owned by a school or music college.

All the above points are important, but if you happen to come across a very good instrument in poor condition, it might be worth your while to spend a bit extra on restoration.

Buying a new instrument

This option should only be pursued if you have been playing for a while and know that you will be carrying on. If money is no object, however, buy the jewel-encrusted, gold-plated number! The best place to start looking would be a specialist wind-instrument store (although it is unlikely to have its most

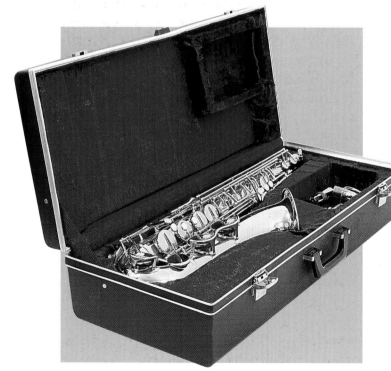

precious instrument in the window) or a general music store. Not all these stores stock clarinets and saxophones, but any worthwhile music establishment should be able to refer you to one that does. Simply not seeing any instruments in the store is not an indication that it doesn't stock them, though. It could have run out of stock or maybe doesn't keep the instruments on the premises but rather in a nearby storage facility. The best way to find out is simply to ask the store attendant or phone before you actually make the trip. Another option is to trawl the Internet for an instrument. If you live in a country that has an effective Internet shopping service, the instrument will be delivered to your door. It's a bit more difficult to return these instruments, though!

If you are lucky to be faced with a wide variety of instruments, you should decide beforehand how much you are willing to spend. What makes it difficult to choose an instrument, especially for the beginner, is that even cheap clarinets and saxophones tend to look good. Usually the price tag will tell you how good the instrument is. Expensive instruments are usually constructed with greater care and use more costly materials.

Take an experienced player along with you. He or she can play the instrument, giving you a chance to listen to its sound. There is also the added benefit of having someone who can give a professional opinion and helpful advice. If you don't know anybody who can play the instrument, another option is to ask if any of the shop assistants do. A good store will usually have musically trained staff who can demonstrate the instruments on sale.

Most stores will also have lay-by systems (after a deposit, they will set aside the instrument until you can fully pay for it and take it away), although with expensive instruments this is not always possible. If an instrument is particularly expensive, a good music shop will allow you to take it away to test it in the comfort of your own home, but it will prefer you to be an experienced player and will usually expect your full details. Expect to pay a deposit in such cases.

Remember also when purchasing a new instrument to ask about a guarantee. Make sure you understand all the conditions of the guarantee before buying. Also ask whether the shop has a policy whereby the instrument gets serviced for free for the first six months or year; they usually do. If they don't, ask for the details of someone who does services and repairs.

If you are serious about playing and have the necessary finances, buying a new instrument is the way to go.

CARING FOR YOUR INSTRUMENT

When you buy a clarinet or saxophone, it is important to view the purchase as a long-term investment. A beginner will usually start on a 'student' instrument and later will upgrade to a more expensive 'professional' one. Looking after your first instrument properly improves its resale value, thereby making the next instrument cheaper. Here are some basic tips to ensure that your instrument remains a good investment:

- Have the instrument serviced at regular intervals; once a year should do the trick. Also ask the person who does the servicing to write a service report so that you can keep an adequate service history, thus improving the resale value.
- If the instrument is new, for the first two months don't play on it for too long at one time, especially if it's a clarinet. The barrel and upper joint have to become accustomed to the change in humidity associated with playing. Playing for too long, especially on a new wooden instrument, may cause cracks in the body.

- Allow your instrument some time out of its case to acclimatize to the temperature of the venue in which you will be playing. If the venue is very cold, you should gradually warm up your instrument with your hands and a few breaths before playing, since dramatic changes in the instrument's temperature could cause the metal to warp or the wood to crack.
- When assembling the instrument, use special cork grease on the joints. This keeps them in good condition and also protects against moisture and humidity. Handle the instrument as gently as possible since too much pressure could damage the key mechanism.
- If you take a break for longer than 10 minutes, rather clean the instrument and put it back in its case. Leaving it outside its case, especially in hot, dry or very cold conditions − or where the temperature fluctuates, such as near a heating device or air conditioner − is not the greatest idea for a sensitive instrument.

ABOVE Cork grease helps to protect the joints (1). Do not leave your instrument lying around near food or drink (2).

ABOVE RIGHT The wisest musician stores his instrument safely in its protective case, out of harm's way.

It's important to have your instrument serviced regularly by a professional if it is to give you long life.

- Do not play directly after eating, as bits of food will get stuck in the bore and mechanism. Always rinse your mouth with water before playing and wash any dirt or sticky substances from your hands.
- Always clean the instrument properly once you've finished playing. Leaving excess moisture inside can cause keys to start sticking or stain, crack or warp the body. It also causes the most horrible smell, which you would rather avoid having near your mouth when you start playing.
- Clean the instrument by disassembling it, then pulling the swab through the body two or three times to remove excess moisture. Also thoroughly clean the mouthpiece, and rinse and dry the reed.
- Wipe the instrument with a soft cloth to remove dust and oil left by your fingers on the keys. This will also stop the keys from becoming sticky and discoloured – and it makes the job of the maintenance expert much easier.
- Do not leave the instrument standing around where it can be stepped on, sat on or knocked over. The best is to store it in its case, leaving this somewhere low where it cannot fall and is safely out of the way of human traffic.
- Do not try to fix anything that is broken since you could do more harm than good. Rather take the instrument to a specialist.

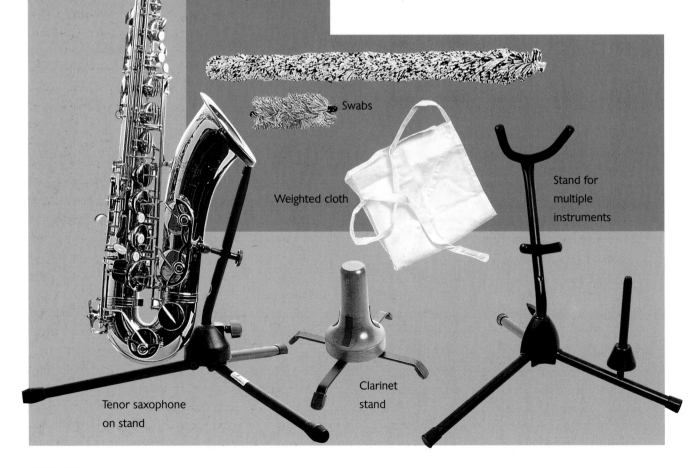

various reed guards

Swabs

Weighted cloth

Stand for multiple instruments

Tenor saxophone on stand

Clarinet stand

BUYING SHEET MUSIC

If you are adept at sight-reading, buying new, untried sheet music can introduce you to many new composers, styles and pieces.

Sheet music refers to printed music. A store that stocks clarinets and saxophones should also have a supply of sheet music available for these instruments. It can also often be found at second-hand shops and garage sales. Having some idea of what music you are looking for helps, alternatively you could browse through the collection on offer at the music store. Here are a few tips to help you negotiate the world of printed music:

• Buy the original sheet music. Playing from photocopies is a violation of copyright and deprives many hard-working typesetters, editors and musicians of their rightful income.

• Look at the music and not just the cover of the book. As a rule, if the music notation looks too 'black' at first sight, it should be avoided until you are more proficient in your playing and sight-reading capabilities. If you are a beginner, scan the music to make sure that it's not beyond your playing range – unless you wish to keep it for later when you are more proficient in playing.

• If you're interested in the music of a certain composer or style, then you should look for anthologies of music; they are often graded in difficulty.

• Don't be restrictive in your tastes of music you buy and play. There is nothing that gives greater pleasure than discovering a beautiful piece of music by accident. Making a habit of reading a lot of music will also improve your sight-reading capabilities.

• If the music store doesn't have the specific sheet music you're looking for, they should be able to order it directly from the publisher. Bear in mind that a handling fee will probably be charged.

• If you buy a piece with accompaniment, make sure you also buy the accompaniment and not just the part for clarinet or saxophone. Usually the accompaniment will have your part printed above it, while your part features only the notes you have to play. Be aware that most pieces for clarinet and saxophone have accompaniment unless they are specified as studies or solos.

• If you play a B-flat clarinet, buying a piece for A-clarinet and piano will not help you since the notes for your part will be transposed incorrectly (although, usually, a piece will have multiple versions of your part for all the different kinds of clarinets or saxophones – but make sure, anyway).

• If you play in a group or ensemble, you should look for music for clarinet or saxophone duets, trios, quartets, and so on. Again, make sure you buy all the parts when purchasing ensemble music, and that they are transposed for the correct instruments in your group.

TAKING LESSONS

Even though you will have gained a lot of tips and advice from this book, you cannot really learn to master an instrument from a book. It is therefore recommended that you find a teacher as soon as you have an instrument and the inclination to take your playing to the next level. Teachers for the clarinet usually also teach and play the saxophone – and vice versa. However, it is important to find a teacher who is passionate about his or her field and creative in its application. A bad teacher can do more harm than good by turning your love for the instrument into an aversion. Here are a few ways to make sure that you get the best possible teacher:

- Phone the teacher and ask whether you can discuss tuition and whether he (or she) is willing to demonstrate his capabilities. If he is offended by you wanting to make comparisons with others, keep looking. The fact remains, you're going to be a paying customer, investing a great deal of money in the long term, so you should have the best 'product' available.
- Ask whether she gives a free first lesson to see whether you are compatible as teacher and student.
- Ask for the teacher's qualifications and credentials. Bear in

mind, however, that just because she passed an exam doesn't mean she's capable of playing well or is enthusiastic and capable of inspiring you as a student.
- Ask about his playing history. Public recitals and other musical activities should be taken into account.
- Remember, however, that many players have opted from the start to specialize in teaching, specifically; in this case, the teacher will be able to teach you many different aspects compared to the specialist performer.
- A good wind-instrument teacher should have sufficient keyboard skills to be able to accompany the pieces you play.
- Do bear in mind that a well-known specialist teacher or recitalist will probably charge more per lesson than his or her obscure counterpart!

This may all seem a little exaggerated, but if you are concerned about the quality of your musical education and do not wish to waste your money and your enthusiasm, heed this advice. Also, bear in mind that learning to play an instrument well can be likened to becoming a world-class athlete: it does not happen overnight, but with the right guidance and tuition – and perseverance – the sky is the limit.

Receiving lessons from a teacher will help correct faulty habits and put your playing on a higher level.

It can give you enormous personal satisfaction to produce harmonious music, together with accomplished musicians.

While it is a rewarding experience to make joyful noise on your own, it is a really exhilarating experience to play with other musicians. Clarinets and saxophones feature in a variety of bands, ensembles and orchestras, and such opportunities to make music together should be fully utilized.

It would help to start by asking your teacher if he could pair you off with another student who is on the same level of proficiency as you. The two of you can start by playing a number of duets. Later, you can ask more people to play with you and you can experiment with a variety of easy ensemble pieces; it's a good way to build confidence playing with others.

One advantage of playing with other musicians is that most people like to stop as soon as they make a mistake, but in this case you cannot afford to stop and are forced to go on. This will also dramatically improve your sight-reading capabilities, which is an essential skill if you want to make music in a group. If you start by playing with people who are more proficient on their instruments than yourself, you are going to feel mightily embarrassed if you can't keep up.

If you have reached a certain level in your playing, you should consider auditioning for a band (see Chapter 5). When you go for the audition, the band master will usually ask you to play something you know, then proceed to making you play an unknown part from sheet music. Obviously, the higher the level of the band, the higher the level of playing they will expect from you. Start by auditioning for amateur bands. If you don't make it, it's not the end of the world, because by the time the next audition happens, your playing will have improved. Apart from being an ideal place to meet new people and socialize, playing in a band or orchestra teaches you some very important lessons in self-discipline and teamwork, which are essential skills in the workplace.

Hopefully, the information, tips and advice set out here will help you make the most of your musical interests.

Accidentals Signs (see: sharp or flat) written before a note to alter the pitch of that note.

Accent A stress on a particular beat or on certain notes, indicated by a symbol printed over the note concerned.

Articulation Signs applied to a note which alter the length of that note; usually pertains to tonguing and breathing, e.g. staccato, tenuto, slur, tie.

Arrangement A piece that has been rescored, rearranged or adapted to be performed in a different way (often for different instruments), not usually by the original composer.

Atonalism/Atonality A system where no key is dominant. It came to the fore in the early 20th century and was pioneered by composers like Arnold Schoenberg.

Bar The division of music into sections. Also, a group of beats that is repeated throughout a piece of music. The number of beats in a bar is indicated by the time signature.

Cantabile Singing, in a singing manner.

Choral(e) Religious songs or hymns that form part of the Protestant liturgy.

Clef A symbol at the beginning of a stave, fixing the pitch of notes according to their position on the stave.

Concert pitch The frequency of 440 hertz (vibrations per second) assigned to the A above middle C.

Counterpoint Music that combines two or more individual melodic lines, or themes, to form a harmonious whole.

Dynamics Variations in volume, from loud to soft. Dynamic marks or markings are the directions and symbols used to indicate degrees of loudness, e.g. *forte, fortissimo, pianissimo, crescendo*.

Fermata A sign (⌒) indicating a pause during a note or rest that is longer than the value to which it applies.

Flat Indicates that the pitch is to be lowered by a semitone, shown by a symbol (♭) placed before a note or in the key signature. Playing flat means too low and out of tune.

Interval The difference of pitch between two notes, calculated by counting the steps on the diatonic scale between the two notes (e.g. the interval between C and G is a fifth).

Key signature The sharps or flats placed after the clef at the beginning of a stave to indicate the prevailing key.

Minuet A stately dance at a moderate tempo with three beats to the bar.

Movement A self-contained section of a larger work. Each movement usually has a separate tempo indication.

Octave An interval of eight notes (twelve semitones) on the diatonic scale.

Ornaments Extra notes (e.g. trills, turns, etc.) added to vocal or instrumental melodies as a decoration or embellishment.

Phrase A group of notes which forms a musical unity.

Pitch The register ('highness' or 'lowness') of a note which determines its position on a stave; measured by the frequency of the vibrations that produce it.

Register The range of an instrument or a singer's voice e.g. tenor, bass, soprano.

Rest A measured silence.

Rhythm The organization of notes in a piece in relation to time. Rhythm is determined by the way the notes are grouped in bars, the number of beats in a bar, and the manner in which the beats are accented.

Sarabande A Spanish courtly dance that is danced in triple time; usually, the second beat is emphasized.

Sforzando An accent indicating that a note needs to be played powerfully.

Sharp A symbol (♯) appearing before a note, or in a key signature, to indicate that the pitch is to be raised by a semitone. Playing or singing 'sharp' means too high – and consequently out of tune.

Song plugger A salesman who promotes a music firm's songs by playing and singing them for potential buyers and performers.

Stave or **staff** A grid of five parallel horizontal lines, and the corresponding spaces between them, on which notes are written. A note's position on the stave determines its relative pitch, with the point of reference indicated by the clef.

Syncopation An accent (or 'off-beat') placed on a normally unaccented beat of a bar (often the second or last beat), to achieve an irregular rhythm. A constant feature of jazz.

Tempo (Italian, 'time'). The speed, or the pace, at which a piece is played, e.g. *presto, andante, adagio*.

Theme A tune, partial tune or recognizable musical entity which forms a central aspect of composition.

Tonality In composition, the basic principle of using a number of keys, one of which is predominant and provides the overall tonality of the music. Compare atonalism.

Tonguing A method used when playing wind instruments to stop the vibrations of the reed with the tip of your tongue.

Transposition Shifting the overall pitch of a piece so it can be performed in a higher or lower key than the original one.

Trill A musical ornament consisting of a rapid alternation between one note and the note above it.

Trio Music for three voices or instruments; also, the middle section of a minuet or scherzo movement.

Triple time Music with three beats to the bar, e.g. a waltz.

Triplet A group of three notes played in the same time allowed for two notes of the same duration.

Variation A modification or development of a theme. Often appears as a 'theme and variations'; a form of movement.

PUBLISHER'S ACKNOWLEDGEMENTS

The author and publisher would like to thank the staff of the Department of Music at the University of Stellenbosch, for their assistance with the photographic shoot; Mr Heuer of Heuer Musikhaus, Stellenbosch for his kind indulgence; Carel van Heerden and the staff of Paul Bothner, Claremont; the staff of the Music Library of the University, Beulah Gericke, Frida Bekker and Yusuf Ras, for their patience and infinite availability and models Mia Martens and Johannes de Jager for their time. The author would like to thank Philip du Toit for his arrangement of the Gershwin piece and Marisa Tolkien for her valuable insight and expertise.

PICTURE CREDITS

p10 (bl) Lebrecht Music/ColouriserAL, (tr) Lebrecht Music Collection. p11 (tr) William Gottlieb/Redferns Music Library, (bl) Lebrecht Music Collection. p17 Lebrecht Music Collection. p24 G Salter/Lebrecht Music Collection. p46 (bl) Musée Nationale de Ceramique, Sevres, France/Bridgeman Art Library, (tr) Lebrecht Music Collection. p47 Lebrecht Music Collection. p48 Lebrecht Music/ColouriserAL. p50 Lebrecht Music Collection. p52 Lebrecht Music Collection. p53 Interfoto, Munich/Lebrecht Music. p54 Lebrecht Music Collection. p56 Lebrecht Music Collection. p58 BM&AG/ Lebrecht Music. p59 Lebrecht Music Collection. p60 Lebrecht Music Collection. p62 Lebrecht Music Collection. p65 Lebrecht Music Collection. p66 Lebrecht Music Collection. p68 galloimages/gettyimages.com. p69 (tl) Lebrecht Music Collection, (br) David Redfern/Redferns Music Library. p70 Lebrecht Music Collection/Richard Haughton. p72 galloimages/gettyimages.com. p75 PhotoAccess/International Stock. p76 Lebrecht Music Collection. p77 Odile Noel/ Lebrecht Music Collection. p78 John R Rifkin/Lebrecht Music Collection. p80 galloimages/gettyimages.com. p81 Fin Costello/Redferns Music Library. p83 Lebrecht Music Collection /ColouriserAL. p90 G Salter/Lebrecht Music Collection. p93 PhotoAccess.

USEFUL WEBSITES

(The websites below were valid at the time of going to print. They offer a starting point for further investigation and no endorsement or recommendation on the part of the author or publisher should be inferred.)

saxophone.org/links
saxshed.com
classicsax.com
saxontheweb.net
saxlessons.com
melmartin.com
dornpub.com
jdhite.com
mouthpieceheaven.com
jodyjazz.com
saxophone.com

welcome.to/saxophoneandclarinet
ocr.woodwind.org
clarinetclassics.com
clarinet-saxophone.asn.av
clarinetandsaxophone.co.uk
geocities.com/saxandclarinet/home.html

GENERAL

andante.com Weekly subscription newsletter providing the latest in classical music news, reviews and commentary.
apassion4jazz.net Styles, milestones, festivals and more.
bbc.co.uk/aboutmusic Artist profiles, news and discographies covering both classical, rock and pop music
history-of-rock.com The golden decade (1955–64).
juilliard.edu/about The Juilliard School, New York.
musicroom.com The world's best music in print.
ram.ac.uk Royal Academy of Music, London.
rcm.ac.uk Royal College of Music, London.
redhotjazz.com Styles, artists, archives.
rollingstone.com Online site of the legendary magazine.
sheetmusicplus.com US-based online store.

ASSOCIATIONS/PUBLICATIONS

The International Clarinet Association – Rose Sperrazza, PO Box 5039, Wheaton, Illinois 60189-5039, USA.
Saxophone Journal (Dorn Publications Inc.), PO Box 206, Medfield, Massachusetts 02052, USA.

FURTHER READING

Baker, Theodore. *Baker's Biographical Dictionary of Musicians*. Revised by Nicholas Slonimsky. Shirmer Books, New York, 1992.

Cummings, David. *Random House Encyclopedic Dictionary of Classical Music*.

Sadie, Stanley (ed.). *The New Grove Dictionary of Music and Musicians*. 2nd edition. Macmillan, 2001. Online subscription version: www.grovemusic.com

Sherman, R. & **Seldon, P.** *The Complete Idiot's Guide to Classical Music*. Alpha Books (A Division of Macmillan Reference, USA), New York, 1997.